Mindfulness for the Next Generation

Mindfulness for the Next Generation

*Helping Emerging Adults
Manage Stress and Lead
Healthier Lives*

Holly Rogers
Margaret Maytan

OXFORD
UNIVERSITY PRESS

OXFORD

UNIVERSITY PRESS

Oxford University Press, Inc., publishes works that further Oxford University's objective
of excellence in research, scholarship, and education.

Oxford New York
Auckland   Cape Town   Dar es Salaam   Hong Kong   Karachi   Kuala Lumpur
Madrid   Melbourne   Mexico City   Nairobi   New Delhi   Shanghai   Taipei   Toronto

With offices in
Argentina   Austria   Brazil   Chile   Czech Republic   France   Greece   Guatemala
Hungary   Italy   Japan   Poland   Portugal   Singapore   South Korea   Switzerland
Thailand   Turkey   Ukraine   Vietnam

Copyright © 2012 by Oxford University Press, Inc.

Published by Oxford University Press, Inc.
198 Madison Avenue, New York, New York 10016
www.oup.com

Oxford is a registered trademark of Oxford University Press, Inc.

Library of Congress Cataloging-in-Publication Data

Rogers, Holly.
  Mindfulness for the next generation : helping emerging adults manage
  stress and lead healthier lives / Holly Rogers, Margaret Maytan.
    p. cm.
  Includes bibliographical references and index.
  ISBN 978-0-19-978257-4
  1. Mindfulness-based cognitive therapy. 2. College students—Mental health.
I. Maytan, Margaret. II. Title.
RC489.M55R64 2012
155.9'042—dc23   2011048700

Printed in the United States of America on acid-free paper

To my most committed and creative teacher of mindfulness, Maggie Rose.—HR

For Gregory, Amelia, Sandra, Rayann, and Nabil, with abiding love. —MM

Contents

Foreword

Mindfulness is a basic human capacity; everyone has the potential to be mindful. Practicing mindfulness involves learning to apply and steady one's attention on the present with curiosity and acceptance. An important focus for mindful awareness is the inner experience of heart, mind, and body.

In this important new book, Holly Rogers and Margaret Maytan share their considerable experience and knowledge of mindfulness practice along with the challenges, rewards, and their own effective methods for teaching mindfulness to college students and other young adults. Holly and Margaret have devoted many years to working with college students and other emerging adults, seeking effective ways to teach their students state-of-the art practices and skills based on mindfulness that will benefit them throughout their lives.

They have named their particular method of teaching mindfulness *Koru*, which is a Maori word for the unfurling fern frond. They chose that image because it symbolizes balanced growth and movement around a center of stable, authentic values. This book is the result of their work and provides a rich resource for anyone who wishes to use mindfulness in his or her work with others, and especially with college students and other emerging adults.

While mindfulness is a basic human capacity and has been promoted and explored extensively by certain traditions—most especially Buddhism—Western psychology, medicine, and science over the past 30 years or so have also become very interested in mindfulness practice and in the healing and transformative potential of mindfulness. A growing body of medical and scientific evidence now exists, testifying to the value of practicing mindfulness for a wide variety of health and psychological conditions and purposes.

A revolution in modern science has occurred in recent years, and we now know that the human brain remains open to change throughout the life span. Research in neuroscience has shown that how one uses one's mind—for example, losing oneself in endless cycles of worried thoughts, cultivating a mental habit of rapidly shifting attention from object to object, or reflecting on a positive quality such as gratitude or generosity—can actually shape the structure and function of the brain. And the way the brain functions can have an enormous impact on well-being, affecting one's health and happiness over the entire life span.

The focus of this book on emerging adulthood (roughly the period of life between ages 18 and 29) is especially important and challenging. Most readers will easily relate to that time when they were no longer adolescents but had not yet fully reached adulthood. It is both an exciting and a challenging time, marked by change and exploration, as well as by deep questioning about sustaining life values, career choices, and relationships.

It is possibly preventive mental health care of the best kind to teach an emerging adult the skills and practices of mindfulness, self-awareness, and self-compassion. Practicing these skills can lead directly to discovery and alignment with one's personal center of stable, authentic values. With increased self-awareness, and with their core values identified and operating, emerging adults are much better equipped to meet life's challenges and opportunities successfully and to take their rightful place in the world. In a time when our culture, our nation, and our world are beset by uncertainties, fears, and anxieties, and many people are searching for stability, authentic values, and ways to be happier and healthier, it is difficult to imagine a better investment than teaching young people mindfulness skills.

I believe we owe Holly and Margaret a deep bow of appreciation for their good work, for their dedication to their students, and for sharing their wisdom by writing this book. They have provided a beautiful map, and guidance for using it, in order to help students, other young adults, and possibly people of all ages, because meeting the challenge of living in accordance with one's authentic values in the context of useful and satisfying relationships is critical at every stage of life.

Jeffrey Brantley, MD, DFAPA
Founding Faculty Member, Duke Integrative Medicine
Founder and Director, Mindfulness-Based Stress
Reduction Program, Duke Integrative Medicine

Author of *Calming Your Anxious Mind* and coauthor with Wendy Millstine of *the five good minutes series, daily meditations for calming your anxious mind,* and *true belonging: mindful practices to help you overcome loneliness, connect with others & cultivate happiness.*

Durham, NC
February 2012

Acknowledgments

I wish to thank Dr. Jeff Brantley, my first mindfulness teacher, who has so generously remained my mentor and friend all these years. My friends at Durham Dharma have kept my meditation practice alive; as I'm constantly saying to my students, I could not have maintained my practice without the support and structure of my sangha. A special thanks to my husband, Bill Price, whose own mindfulness practice is a constant source of inspiration to me.

Our meditation program and this book owe much to Dr. Kathy Hollingsworth, the former executive director of Duke's Counseling and Psychological Services (CAPS). Kathy believed in our work and made sure we had the money, time, and space we needed to build our program. Dr. Kelly Crace, our current executive director, has also provided unwavering support for our program. His expertise on the importance of values clarification for emerging adults has helped guide my thinking about the importance of mindfulness training for this group. I am grateful for the support and guidance of both of these excellent leaders.

I am fortunate in my work and particularly blessed by wonderful colleagues at CAPS, all of whom have supported my mindfulness work. I am especially appreciative of Dr. Gary Glass' organizational assistance and the steadfast encouragement of my dear friend Libby Webb. And of course, a very special thanks to my coauthor and coteacher, Margaret, whose creativity and warmth enliven everything she does.

Finally, it is with the deepest gratitude and respect that I wish to thank all the Duke students who have come through our meditation program. It is a privilege to share in their transformation; much that I know about life I learned from them.—HR

My path toward mindfulness began in 1993 when my friend Jane Dyer handed me a book by Anthony de Mello called *Awareness.* Jane has mentored me ever since, and I am deeply grateful. My mindfulness practice has not only transformed my everyday life but also enriched my love and understanding of the Baháʼí Writings, the center of my spiritual life.

Kathryn Connor, M.D., introduced me to the programs at the Center for Mind–Body Medicine and made it possible for me to attend. Together, we started mind–body skills groups at Duke University Medical Center. Thanks, Kathy! And a big thanks goes to James S. Gordon, M.D., who has been a constant source of support and an inspiring model. I have had the good fortune to have him as my supervisor during all of my training.

Holly and I are both grateful to Kathy Hollingsworth, Ph.D., the former executive director of Duke's Counseling and Psychological Services, who has wholeheartedly supported our courses.

Holly's and my work together—our teaching and our writing—has been a source of deep satisfaction and joy to me. Thank you, Holly, for your wisdom and your kind heart.

And, lastly, my deep appreciation to our students for inspiring me and teaching me throughout the years!—MM

Introduction

Most of us can clearly remember how it felt to be going off to college or deciding what career to pursue. Perhaps you remember feeling lost or pressured as you struggled to find direction in life. You can also probably recall some of the sharp pains of love lost or unrequited as you searched for that perfect life partner. These major transitions offer opportunities for growth, even transformation, especially if young adults, or *emerging adults*, as we call them, can tap into their core values and act with authenticity and wisdom. Unfortunately, these days many emerging adults feel so lost and pressured that they are not able to experience any meaningful personal growth. Fortunately, there is a tool—mindfulness—that can help them find solid ground to stand on while their development unfolds.

Mindfulness, as defined by Dr. Jon Kabat-Zinn, is "learning to pay attention, without judgment, to your present-moment experience" (1994, p. 4). Perhaps somewhat surprisingly, simply learning to keep one's attention focused in the present moment has profound positive consequences for our physical and mental health. Also surprisingly, little has been written about the best way to teach this important skill to emerging adults; in our experience, traditional methods for teaching mindfulness and meditation are not always effective for individuals in this stage of development.

Using mindfulness as an approach to managing stress and enhancing the quality of life has become wildly popular in this country. It is likely, since you are reading this book, that you have heard of or already practiced some form of mindfulness. Programs such as Dr. Kabat-Zinn's Mindfulness-Based Stress Reduction and Dr. James S. Gordon's Center for Mind–Body Medicine have brought mindfulness-based practices into the mainstream. Many American adults are practicing and benefiting from these approaches, and we have found that young adults also stand to gain a great deal when they start developing the habit of mindfulness.

Over the last few years, there has been a growing awareness of the unique challenges faced by young people in the developmental stage that is coming to be known as *emerging adulthood*. Dr. Jeffrey Jensen Arnett coined this term in reference to young adults from about ages 18 to 25 and has identified the particular characteristics of this developmental phase (Arnett, 2000). More recently, Arnett and others have recognized that this stage may last even longer, up to age 29. These characteristics will be reviewed in detail in chapters 1 and 2, but in brief, the stage is characterized by a strong drive for identity development in the context of multiple life choices and transitions. It has become apparent in recent years that this age group is facing unique challenges, and many of these young people are becoming overwhelmed by the associated stress. Crises on university campuses, including tragedies such as the Virginia Tech massacre in 2007 and suicide epidemics at some elite universities, have evoked demands from everyone from parents to politicians that something be done to help our young adults manage this time of growth and change. As psychiatrists with years of experience practicing and teaching mindfulness skills and meditation, we felt that one obvious solution was to apply the theory and strategy of mindfulness to the challenges of emerging adulthood.

Our model for teaching mindfulness and meditation grew out of our early failed attempts to engage emerging adults in mindfulness training. Before our paths converged in 2005, we had both sought ways to bring these life-changing practices to emerging adults. In 1996, one of us (Holly Rogers) began working as a staff psychiatrist at Duke University's student counseling center. Holly observed high levels of anxiety and stress in the students she worked with; in an effort to help them manage their distress, she began teaching classes in mindfulness meditation. She observed that it was fairly easy to get the students to sign up for the classes, but the attrition rate was high; by the end of the year, only a few students had begun to incorporate a mindfulness practice into their lives on a regular basis. These initial classes were taught according to more traditional models of meditation instruction, which did not seem to engage the students in any meaningful way. Eventually, it became clear that a whole new approach was needed.

As Holly was beginning to rethink her way of teaching her meditation classes, she met Margaret Maytan. Margaret, also a Duke psychiatrist, had been teaching mind–body skills to faculty, staff, and physicians-in-training at Duke University Medical Center. Her classes with the physicians-in-training had also led her to the knowledge that a different model was needed for this younger age group.

Margaret's training and experience were in facilitating mind–body skills groups using the model created by Dr. Gordon at his Center for Mind–Body Medicine. In this model, small groups meet weekly for 8 weeks to learn and process different stress management and self-awareness skills, including mindfulness, as well as belly breathing, dynamic breathing, guided imagery, and others. What Margaret had quickly learned in teaching these classes at the Medical Center was that highly stressed physicians-in-training have difficulty following through with an 8-week training program. There was a high drop-off rate for trainee groups, whereas the groups composed of faculty and social workers were much more successful. Even when the number of classes in the course was reduced, the physicians-in-training just could not commit to the program. Like Holly, Margaret was trying to figure out a better way to teach mindfulness to highly stressed young people.

We decided to collaborate and began putting together a model for teaching mindfulness to university students. Our program has come to be known as "Koru: An Introduction to Mindfulness and Meditation for Duke Students," or just "Koru." *Koru* is a Maori word that literally means "looped" or "spiraled," and it refers to the spiral shape of the unfurling fern fronds that are so abundant in the Maoris' homeland of New Zealand. A Koru is a meaningful symbol for the Maori people, symbolizing new life, growth, balance, and harmony. The Koru is a natural representation of the ideal balance between new growth and stability, the balance we promote for our students. We have seen this balance develop in our students, and invariably it has led them toward greater wisdom and confidence as they navigate the challenges of emerging adulthood.

The approach we use with Koru has evolved from our personal experiences of practicing and teaching mindfulness, as well as our understanding of the developmental characteristics and needs of emerging adults. The program teaches traditional mindfulness meditation practices as well as some of the mind–body skills from Margaret's training.

In the fall of 2005 we piloted our first class and were very pleased with the results. The students enthusiastically engaged with us throughout the course and at the end reported how helpful the experience had been. Much to our surprise, we were soon trying to manage long waiting lists of students who had heard about the course and wanted to attend.

We suspect that the success of our model is driven by two primary factors. First, there is an excellent fit between the drive for identity development in emerging adults and the self-knowledge evoked by mindfulness practices. Second, our approach takes into account the characteristic attitudes, perspectives, needs, and goals of typical university students.

Over the years we have experimented with our model, adjusting different variables such as class size, the number of classes, and the length of classes. We have also experimented with different approaches for teaching mindfulness to this group, as we found that what worked for older adults did not necessarily capture the interest of our students. We have finally achieved what we believe to be the most effective model for teaching mindfulness to emerging adults and are now eager to share what we have learned with others wishing to teach this dynamic and interesting age group.

Mindfulness for the Next Generation: Helping Emerging Adults Manage Stress and Lead Healthier Lives is a book that will hopefully inspire you to begin teaching mindfulness to the emerging adults in your life, and it will give you all the tools you need to start teaching Koru. The book is designed primarily to be a guide and manual for those individuals who wish to begin teaching mindfulness to college students or other young adults. We have specifically organized the material to make it possible for almost anybody with experience practicing mindfulnes to effectively teach Koru's mindfulness-based coping strategies and meditations. In chapter 3 of the book, we describe general teaching strategies that are effective for teaching mindfulness to emerging adults. Chapter 4 reviews some of the scientific research behind mindfulness meditation and mind–body skills. Chapter 5 contains all the information you will need to organize your own Koru program. Chapters 6 through 9 serve as a manual for teaching each of the program's four classes. Although the model has been designed for emerging adults and tested on university students, it likely would also work well for older adolescents and other young adults.

Whether you are a mental health professional, a school administrator, or a peer facilitator, you can use the information in these pages to develop a successful Koru program at your school, agency, or organization. If, on the other hand, you are a stressed-out emerging adult looking for a healthier way to manage your life, this book will provide all the information you need to bring mindfulness into your life in a meaningful way.

During the time that we have been teaching mindfulness to university students, we have been privileged to observe growth and transformation that surprised even us. We have taken over 300 students through the course, and their feedback has been overwhelmingly positive. They tell us that they have developed the ability to practice mindfulness in their daily lives and that, as a result, they are getting in touch with something profound within themselves that is changing the way they view the world and their place in it. They have also shared with us important improvements in their ability to manage their stress, worry, and anxiety. It has become increasingly clear to us that we have developed an effective model for helping emerging adults cope with their important struggles and lead healthier lives.

Our wish now is to expand the number of young adults in our communities who have access to the life-enhancing benefits of mindfulness and meditation. In the service of that goal, we have created this book to share our hard-earned experience in teaching mindfulness to emerging adults. Throughout the text, we have tried to bring our students' voices to life by relying on questions and comments taken from three sources:

- Students' typical comments and questions during class
- E-mails from students
- Anonymous written evaluations provided at the end of the course

We have been careful to use fictionalized names and to remove any identifying information from the quotes. For e-mails from individuals, we have paraphrased the text so that the authors would not be identifiable. No individual student should be recognizable, but because students have common experiences and struggles, these quotes will most certainly seem familiar to anyone who has been through one of our courses.

We hope that our joy in this work will shine through the chapters that follow, but above all, we hope that our model can assist others in their work with this age group to enrich and transform their lives. Welcome to Koru!

PART ONE

Teaching Mindfulness to College Students and Other Emerging Adults

Koru

A New Model

The faculty of voluntarily bringing back a wandering attention,
over and over again, is the very root of judgement, character, and will.
No one is *compos sui* if he have it not.
An education which should improve this faculty
Would be the education par excellence.
But it is easer to define this ideal
Than to give practical instructions for bringing it about.
    WILLIAM JAMES, *Principles of Psychology* (1890)

I have found that mindfulness has pervaded my life. On and off I realize that
my mind is spinning and it has become much easier for me to take some
breaths and bring my mind back to the present. I have found I'm worrying less
because I have better control over my mind.
    DUKE STUDENT AFTER TAKING THE KORU MINDFULNESS CLASS

The bells in Duke Chapel ring out across campus for 15 minutes every day at 5 o'clock. At the same time on most Tuesdays during the academic year, a group of students make their way to the counseling center, next door to the chapel, to participate in a course on mindfulness and meditation. The students are a diverse group racially and ethnically, and they are male and female, gay and straight, U.S. nationals and foreign nationals. There are undergraduates and graduate students. At various times, virtually all of Duke's professional schools are represented, as medical students, law students, divinity students, business students, and nursing students come to learn about mindfulness and about how to better manage their stress and anxiety. The students come to this course having been referred by a counselor, by coming across the ad in the student newspaper or on the counseling center's web site, or just by hearing through the grapevine that it's a

MINDFULNESS FOR THE NEXT GENERATION: THE COURSE ESSENTIALS

Course Title: Koru: An introduction to mindfulness and meditation for students. (Of course, you can change *students* to any word that best describes your participants.)

Required Text: *Wherever You Go, There You Are* by Jon Kabat-Zinn

Setting: A room large enough to hold comfortably up to 14 chairs in a circle.

Teachers: Koru can be taught by one person, but the content will be a bit richer if you have two teachers. Some experience with mindfulness practice is essential.

Participants: The course was developed for emerging adults and tested on university students. It will probably also work well for late adolescents and nonstudent emerging adults.

Class Size: Twelve participants are optimal. Four to 14 will work.

Course Structure: Four 75-minute classes spaced over 4–5 weeks. Each class follows the same format: opening meditation, check-in, skill training, closing meditation. The format is described in detail in chapter 5. The individual meditations and skills are described in detail in chapters 6–9.

Course Materials:

A bell or chime to signal the beginning and end of meditation periods

A music player of some sort

Recorded guided meditations to give to students (optional)

Course syllabus (appendix B)

The log for students to record their homework (appendix C)

Copies of the gatha to give to students (for the second class; see chapter 7)

Raisins or grapes (for the fourth class)

Class evaluation (for the fourth class; appendix F)

Resource guide for students (appendix E)

---

useful experience. Almost all are feeling pressured and stressed, worried about keeping up with all the demands they are facing. They may feel that they are not functioning academically as well as they would like. Most have had no prior exposure to or experience of mindfulness and come to the class hopeful and curious, eager to learn but perhaps also a little skeptical.

At the end of the 4-week course, a large majority of these students report that they have been transformed by the experience. They say that they now have found ways to enjoy their lives more fully and also to cope with their stress. They feel better able to handle their work and are optimistic about their future.

Leah and Phillip are typical of the students who come to the mindfulness and meditation course.

Leah, an Undergraduate

Leah is a 19-year-old college sophomore. In high school, Leah excelled as a student and was active in sports and student government. She had many friends. She worked hard to get into a good college and felt confident that she would do well. She anticipated that her time in college would be an exciting and fun-filled adventure.

When she arrived at Duke, she couldn't believe her good fortune. The campus was beautiful, and she immediately began to make new friends. Her classes were interesting but also tougher than she'd anticipated. Despite long hours of study, her grades at the end of her freshman year were not as good as she'd expected, and she was tired and stressed. She began to worry about her future plans to attend law school.

By the time Leah returned to Duke to start her sophomore year, she was dreading school. She had a knot in her stomach every time she thought about it, she kept getting a lot of colds, and she was sleeping poorly. She no longer noticed the beautiful campus, and it was hard for her to enjoy her time with her friends. She no longer felt that she could, or even wanted to, pursue the goals she'd originally set for herself. She felt pressured and lost. She realized that she needed to figure out a better strategy for dealing with the competing pressures of school.

Phillip, a Graduate Student

Phillip is a 25-year-old Ph.D. candidate in the Department of Microbiology. Phillip entered graduate school confident that he wanted to be a biological scientist, and the first 2 years went well. However, 3 years into the program, he began to question all of his choices. His work in the lab was not going well, and his adviser was generally unavailable and unhelpful. He regretted choosing this lab and even choosing Duke. His work lost meaning for him. He and his girlfriend started to talk about a future together, but she was finding his lack of motivation and indecision difficult to live with. As the pressure built at work and in his relationship, he submitted to the temptation to avoid his worries by playing computer games and staying out late drinking with friends.

Although Leah and Phillip are in different stages of their academic careers, they are dealing with similar stressors. There are many different ways to conceptualize their problems, but one factor they have in common is that they are both struggling with issues related to identity and authenticity. They are trying unsuccessfully to manage these typical developmental struggles by rethinking past choices and worrying about future directions. Coping strategies such as avoiding the underlying issues by either working obsessively or not working at all only add to the problem. Both of these students are aware that they need help, and it is often these kinds of students who turn to our class.

We have developed a model, which we call *Koru*, for teaching the practice of mindfulness and the learning of mindfulness-based stress-management strategies to students like Leah and Phillip who are having trouble coping with the developmental tasks of emerging adulthood. This model, which consists of four 75-minute classes, has proven to be very effective in helping to guide students through these challenging times. This book is designed to provide anyone working with individuals in the emerging adulthood phase of development all the information needed to create a similar program. However, even if you want to learn mindfulness and meditation only for your own personal development, you will find this book a useful introduction and guide to these life-enhancing practices.

Emerging Adults

The period of life from roughly age 18 to age 29 has been termed *emerging adulthood* (Arnett, 2000). Men and women in this stage are no longer adolescents, nor have they moved fully into adulthood. Emerging adulthood is an exciting and unique time of life. It is a time of change and exploration of possible life directions. Emerging adults are beginning to struggle with important life choices. What career is best for them? Who is the right life partner for them? What measures of success are important to them? The constraints of childhood have generally fallen away, but these young people have not yet acquired fully the adult responsibilities of family and career that provide boundaries and limits. During this stage, there are fewer restrictions and more opportunities to explore than during any other time of life.

Emerging adulthood naturally comes with a lot of uncertainty. Most of the questions about future paths are not yet answered, and the options can seem unlimited. The lack of limitations itself can sometimes add to the confusion. It is not uncommon to hear emerging adults say, "I wish I didn't have so many choices. I just wish someone would tell me what to do." Of course, they would object if we did tell them what to do, but at times the variety of options to choose from can leave them feeling stuck and overwhelmed. The message that "you can do anything" may be heard as "you should do everything," a tough standard to live up to. They fear both not trying, and trying and failing.

All of this change and opportunity for exploration comes with a great deal of pressure and stress, particularly for the generation of students born between 1980 and 2000 (Howe & Strauss, 2000), known as the *millennials* or the *tragedy generation*. These young people came of age during the period of the 9/11 terrorist attacks and the subsequent "war on terror." They were highly sheltered and the focus of intense safety concerns. They tend to have been pushed and pressured by parents to a greater degree than previous generations. Compared to earlier generations they have had less free time, and their youth has often been taken up with activities in the service of their—or their parents'—future aspirations. Thus, many of these emerging adults arrive at this stage of development feeling an obligation to succeed but lacking the inner resources they need to manage the competing pressures they face and to make wise choices for themselves.

Therefore, emerging adults in general, but particularly this generation of college students, are struggling to balance the freedom of choice and opportunity with their expectation of success and fear of failure. Of course, not all emerging adults attend colleges or universities, but a large and growing percentage do. According to the National Center for Education Statistics, enrollment in degree-granting institutions increased by 26% between 1996 and 2007, from 14.5 million to 18.2 million (U.S. Department of Education, 2009).

Interestingly, emerging adults recognize that what makes them not quite adults is their immaturity. They perceive the attainment of adulthood as being marked not by objective measures such as career and family, but instead by subjective measures such as self-sufficiency and independent decision making (Arnett, 2000). Essentially, they recognize that a certain level of maturity and wisdom is what will make them adult, and they know they have not yet achieved it.

Mindfulness, which we'll explain further below, can play a valuable role here, helping students to tolerate uncertainty and develop wisdom by tapping into the resources that are available within all of us. Learning simple calming skills such as deep belly breathing or guided imagery can empower them to feel that they can calm themselves quickly in stressful situations. Meditation, even in small amounts, can help students feel more grounded and focused. We cannot overstate the potentially profound impact of developing, at this critical time of life, a mindfulness practice that includes mindfulness-based stress-management skills and meditation.

Mindfulness and Meditation

Mindfulness is simply a way of learning to live more fully in the present. It is the practice of becoming more aware and engaged in every moment of our lives by bringing our attention, with curiosity and acceptance, to bear on our present-moment experience. With mindfulness practice we learn to release our worries about the future, release our regrets about the past, and focus with a sense of calm acceptance on the present moment. Mindfulness develops what is known as the *observing mind*, the state of consciousness that allows us to have a broader, yet more grounded perspective on our life experiences. By practicing mindfulness and meditation we can learn to see our lives more clearly, and we are able to find ways to bring pleasure and interest more fully into our daily experiences. We can begin to see that often our thoughts about our experiences—rather than the experiences themselves—produce much of our stress and anxiety. As we practice this way of being in the world, we find that we gradually begin to experience more peace and less worry in our lives; a sense of balance unfolds. Practicing mindfulness involves developing certain qualities of mind including wisdom, patience, and compassion, qualities that are particularly important to emerging adults as they try to navigate their way into adulthood.

Before we proceed, a brief comment about our choice of terminology may be helpful. When referring to our curriculum, we typically use the phrase *mindfulness and meditation* rather than the more common phrase *mindfulness meditation.* The latter term refers to a specific type of meditation, which is in fact the type of meditation we teach in our course. However, we want to emphasize that we teach a range of mindfulness skills, not just mindfulness meditation. In order to make this clear, we have chosen to use the more accurate, if slightly more cumbersome, phrase *mindfulness and meditation.*

Mindfulness, Meditation, and the Emerging Adult

College and university students, and everyone else, for that matter, notice that when they stop and pay attention for a moment, there is often a disconnect between their bodies and their minds. For example, if we ask people, "Where is your mind when you're taking a shower, brushing your teeth, or walking to class?" we typically hear that their minds are somewhere else—worrying, making plans, remembering some past problem, passing judgment on themselves or someone else. In this way, they go through their days not even noticing the vast majority of everyday experiences. Often only novel or particularly unpleasant events penetrate their fog of future-oriented thoughts. This approach to life can rob them of their experience of some of the best things about being alive. Even worse for emerging adults, it can block their access to their authentic desires and innate wisdom, hampering their ability to find a coherent path for themselves. Mindfulness is about learning to bridge the mind–body disconnect, to begin to make contact with what is true and wise and kind within all of us and to use this knowledge to move confidently into the future.

From the emerging adults we teach, we hear in various ways about the impact of their developing mindfulness. For example, one student observed that her worries about her grades receded when she paid attention to the autumnal colors on the trees while walking to class. Another student noticed that she was falling asleep more easily since she began appreciating the warmth and comfort of her bed instead of thinking of all the tasks ahead of her the next day. Still another student found that he felt less distracted in class when he developed the intention to listen closely to the professor's lecture. These moments of clear awareness tend to be very meaningful to our students, revealing to them that there truly is a different way to experience their full and busy lives.

Koru: Bringing Emerging Adults and Mindfulness Together

As we often tell our students, mindfulness is simple but very hard to learn. Students live in a high-tech world that involves constant multitasking and productivity. They write their papers while Facebooking, Twittering, and texting, with music blaring through their ear buds. Convincing them that less is more is a monumental task. That there is value in just sitting still and observing their breathing runs counter to their view of the world.

Yet, students who learn and experience mindfulness meditation see quickly how it can truly transform them, helping them to meet life's ups and downs with more peace of mind.

Emerging adults—and, indeed, most of us—also need ways to cope quickly with sudden challenges, such as overwhelming anxiety and severe stress. College students live with large demands on them, both from the world around them and from their own internalized expectations; they need tools to help them cope. Stress-management tools, also known as *mind–body skills*, are based on the core elements of mindfulness. These tools, such as guided imagery and deep belly breathing, can play an important role in decreasing the feeling of stress and increasing the sense of peace and calm.

We have learned that although the benefits of learning mindfulness and mind–body skills are clear to those of us who teach them, our students don't always come easily to this understanding. We can talk endlessly about the benefits of mindfulness, but if we can't convince them to try it, to experience it for themselves, we are never going to impact their behavior and their experience of stress.

After a significant amount of trial and error, plus a fair amount of thought about the developmental imperatives of this age group, we developed Koru. *Koru* is the name we have chosen for our program, because the word is emblematic of the transformation we guide our students toward. *Koru* is the Maori word for the spiral shape of the unfurling fern frond. It symbolizes new, developing life as well as balance, harmony, and stability and thus reflects the essence of what we believe to be most important for our emerging adults.

The program has proven to be quite successful in helping our students integrate the core features of mindfulness into their lives. We have found that a combination of meditation and specific calming skills is most effective. For example, some students find sitting meditation too difficult in the beginning. It might make them too sleepy or too anxious or restless. Our goal is to give them a mindfulness tool that will work for them. Maybe walking meditation or dynamic breathing, two skills that we teach, will be the best place for an exhausted student to start. At the same time, we use guided sitting meditation in class to allow them to experience directly the benefits of focusing their attention on the present moment and calming their bodies and minds.

A central feature of our class is the mutual learning in a small group. Through sharing their experiences as they learn the skills, the students teach each other and enrich each other's practice. The group is not a process group, and the students are not encouraged to talk about their life problems in great detail. Instead, they are encouraged to talk about the challenges and rewards they've experienced with their mindfulness and skills practice over the previous week; questions or problems with their practice are quickly addressed as we work to remove obstacles to their progress. Nearly all of the teaching about mindfulness is done through this process of *checking in*, using the struggles and examples the students bring us to illuminate and clarify the essential features of mindfulness.

Students at this stage of development often benefit from having clearly stated external expectations in place. If there is no deadline and a task is not required, they are unlikely to give it priority. Thus, Koru has mandatory attendance, required reading, and homework that consists of 10 minutes of mindfulness skills practice each day. We have created a special log for the students that includes space for recording their daily skills practice and space for recording their daily gratitude practice (see chapter 6). This log must be completed and returned to class each week. Most of the students complete all of the class requirements and report that they find the structure helpful.

Who Can Teach This Course?

We believe that almost anyone will be able to teach our course on mindfulness, provided that he or she is willing to carefully read this book and spend time developing his or her own mindfulness practice. No particular credentials are needed to teach this course. Familiarity with some form of mindfulness practice is needed, but advanced training in meditation is not necessary. You might be a teaching assistant, a psychologist, a clinical social worker, a church group leader, a counselor at a college, a resident adviser, or a graduate or undergraduate student. The only requirement is a willingness to spend time understanding and practicing the concepts and skills that we teach. The entire course can be taught by a single teacher, but it is helpful to have two teachers leading and responding to the students' questions.

Traditionally, mindfulness and meditation are taught only by practitioners of the art, and there are some good reasons for this. It can be hard to convincingly convey the benefits of mindfulness or to understand the challenges if you haven't experienced them for yourself. However, our aim is to make our course accessible to as many young adults as possible, so in this book we have tried to provide the information and resources you need to get started as a teacher, even if you do not have extensive experience practicing mindfulness or meditation.

Before you begin teaching, we recommend that you carefully study this book and the required text for the course, Kabat-Zinn's *Wherever You Go, There You Are* (1994). Additionally, we suggest that while you are teaching a course, you commit to the same homework you give your students: a minimum of 10 minutes a day of practicing meditation or one of the mindfulness skills taught in the Koru course. If you don't already have some form of mindfulness practice, you will want to develop your own practice before you begin teaching. If you intend to further develop your skills as a mindfulness teacher, it will be important for you to deepen your own experience with mindfulness and meditation.

To make it possible for someone relatively new to mindfulness to teach our course effectively, we have included a great deal of detailed information to guide and support you as you get started. In chapters 6 through 9, we provide scripts for teaching the mindfulness skills and leading the meditations in each class. You'll find detailed answers for the questions students typically ask, and examples of stories and metaphors we find helpful for conveying the important features of mindfulness. As you begin to teach, you will likely discover, as we have, that your mindfulness practice enhances your teaching and your teaching inspires your practice.

Back to Leah and Phillip

If we consider again the situations of Leah and Phillip, we can see how training in mindfulness and meditation could be helpful to them.

Leah is on a quickly moving treadmill that is powered mostly by her future-oriented worries. She is so concerned about what may happen in the future if she doesn't perform well today that she can't look calmly and realistically at her current life situation. Her anxiety is at times overwhelming, and she has difficulty sleeping.

She will likely benefit from:

- Deep belly breathing before sleep
- Guided meditations to calm herself before sleep and as part of her daily practice (the students are given recorded meditations to assist with their homework)
- Learning in class how to be in the moment with her body's sensations as a way to break the cycle of her mind's worries
- Observing her anxious thoughts and trying not to judge them
- Trying dynamic breathing or mindful walking to get relief from the pressure of her worries and thoughts

Leah will learn about the paradox of nonstriving, which we'll talk more about later (see chapter 3). We will help her start to see the richness and beauty in her life and encourage her to intentionally bring her awareness to these qualities on a daily basis. Through all of these practices, Leah will likely begin to develop greater patience with herself and feel less pressured. She will have a greater sense of well-being and improved academic performance, short-term goals that she values.

Phillip has lost sight of his vision for his future life, and because of this, he can't deal with the day-to-day tasks and choices that are important to his progress. His disappointment with his lack of progress is causing him to doubt his choices. Rather than allowing himself to rest fully in the wisdom of the present moment, he oscillates between regret about past choices and worry about future events. When these issues become overwhelming he just avoids them, which puts him further behind and further from clarity about his best path.

For Phillip, these practices might be helpful:

- Meditation to help him develop greater self-understanding
- Walking meditation for those times when he is too restless to sit

- Deep belly breathing as a way to tolerate staying present
- Guided imagery for self-calming
- The practice of nonjudging to help him have compassion for himself

Phillip will learn to see more clearly the obstacles that are interfering with his progress in the lab. He will probably start to observe that patterns of behavior, triggered by emotional reactivity, have the potential to be changed, moment by moment. We will teach Phillip about *acceptance*, being careful to distinguish it from *passive resignation*, a concept that emerging adults dislike. He will learn that staying present is ultimately the surest path to effective problem solving, and that will enable him to make wise choices for himself. The daily gratitude practice will help him become more aware of the world around him, broaden his perspective, and improve his optimism. Through all of these practices, Phillip will likely begin to feel more present and effective in his work and more confident about his choices.

Our Vision

Have you ever had the experience of stopping so completely,
of being in your body so completely,
of being in your life so completely,
that what you knew and what you didn't know,
that what had been and what was yet to come,
and the way things are right now
No longer held even the slightest hint of anxiety or discord?
It would be a moment of complete presence, beyond striving, beyond mere acceptance,
beyond the desire to escape or fix anything or plunge ahead,
a moment of pure being, no longer in time,
a moment of pure seeing, pure feeling,
a moment in which life simply is,
and that "isness" grabs you by all your senses,
all your memories, by your very genes,
by your loves, and
welcomes you home.

Jon Kabat-Zinn, *Coming to Our Senses* (2005), p. 243.
Copyright ©2005 Jon Kabat-Zinn, Ph.D. Reprinted by
Permission of Hyperion. All Rights Reserved.

It is hard to imagine what it is like for stressed and anxious college and university students to experience what Kabat-Zinn is talking about. But we see it over and over again in their faces when they have caught a glimpse, felt it in their deepest selves, and know that such presence is possible. Over the last several years, we have been profoundly touched by the transformation we have seen in the students who have participated in our classes. Over the course of just 4 weeks, we observe peace and wisdom emerging in young people who have great potential just waiting to develop, potential that is often limited by stress, anxiety, and worry. We envision students who take into the world and into their workplaces greater compassion, an openness to whatever is happening in the present, a sense of gratitude, and a belief in themselves and their ability to cope with the challenges of life. These students will make wiser choices as they navigate their career paths, their relationships, and their responsibilities to the world around them. It is our hope that by sharing the wisdom obtained from our own teaching experience, we can encourage others to join us in the very rewarding work of helping emerging adults integrate the gift of mindfulness into their developmental process.

How does mindfulness training help bring emerging adults "home" to themselves, as Kabat-Zinn says above? In the next chapter, we'll learn more about people in this age group and why mindfulness can have such a profound impact on their lives.

More about Emerging Adults and Mindfulness

The underlying premise of our model is that the developmental characteristics of emerging adults make them especially well suited to benefit from mindfulness and meditation. At the same time, these developmental characteristics strongly influence the way emerging adults respond when learning mindfulness; as a result, traditional models for teaching mindfulness may be ineffective. In this chapter, we will explore more fully the characteristics of the emerging adult developmental stage and begin to understand some of the pressures that arise during this interesting time of life. We'll also reflect on the benefits of mindfulness training and see why this practice can be so useful for individuals progressing through this period of development.

Emerging Adults: Who Are They, Really?

Jeffrey Jensen Arnett, who coined the term *emerging adults* and who has done the most work on identifying the characteristics of this age group, articulates five main features of emerging adulthood (2000, 2004). Table 2.1 shows these features, as well as related developmental tasks and questions that we see our students trying to address. As Arnett describes it, emerging adulthood is a relatively new developmental stage, a product of changing culture in the developed world. With this change in culture, the age of marriage and parenthood has moved to a later time in life. This delay in the onset of adult family responsibilities contributes to a delay in other aspects of development as well, especially the need to make early decisions about work and career choices. As a result, the period of life from about age 18 to age 29, which used to be the time for starting careers and raising young children, has now become a time that is open, free of adult responsibilities, and ripe for exploration and self-discovery.

Arthur W. Chickering (1969; Chickering & Reisser, 1993) articulated an earlier psychosocial model of the development of college students. His model also emphasized the search for identity that is typical of this age group. He described seven *vectors* of

CHAPTER 2: KEY POINTS

- The developmental characteristics of emerging adults make them especially well suited to benefit from mindfulness and meditation.
- Emerging adults have the task of developing their identity by clarifying their values and making choices about careers and life partners.
- The array of choices and perceived expectations create a sense of extreme pressure and stress for many emerging adults.
- Mindfulness assists with the developmental tasks of emerging adulthood by providing relief from pressure and worry.
- Perhaps even more important, mindfulness allows students to develop greater self-knowledge and provides a framework they can use to evaluate their life choices.

student development: developing competence, moving through autonomy toward independence, developing mature interpersonal relationships, developing purpose, establishing identity, managing emotions, and developing integrity. Although Chickering's model has some different emphases, like Arnett's emerging adult model it highlights the seeking, questing nature of this time of life. Emerging adults are seekers.

In our work with college and university students, we have found that there are certain questions that naturally emerge for them. What do I value? What will make me happy? What sort of work will be meaningful for me? What sort of person do I want to become? What sort of person will make a good partner for me? From Table 2.1, we can see that these questions correspond to the developmental characteristics and tasks of emerging adulthood; finding answers to these questions is an integral part of the journey through this stage of development.

As emerging adults move through their 20s, they seek to answer these questions and to resolve the uncertainties on their path to full adulthood. This involves a fair amount of experimentation as they develop relationships, explore different career ideas, and seek to clarify their values in general. Frequent transitions are a necessary component of this time of development, and transitions can produce a sense of instability, even anxiety at times, as the emerging adults strive to know themselves better and to make choices based on this self-knowledge. Emerging adults value happiness and see it as a goal that is worth working for (Arnett, 2004, pp. 180–182), but they aren't quite sure how to achieve it. In our classes at Duke, we have found that students respond strongly to the word *authenticity*: they are searching for the life path that feels authentic and right for them. In other words, they are seeking wisdom.

TABLE 2.1 Features and Tasks of Emerging Adulthood and the Self-knowledge Needed to Aid in Navigating through This Stage

Feature of Emerging Adulthood*	Related Task	Self-knowledge Goals
Emphasis on identity exploration.	Clarify values and beliefs.	Who am I? What do I value?
Instability and frequent changes in many spheres of life.	Explore a variety of living situations, jobs, partners, educational goals.	What path most suits me?
Focused on self, making choices based on personal desires since there are few commitments to others.	Develop goals and relationships based on personal preferences.	What do I want? What will make me happy?
Feeling in between adolescence and adulthood, not yet fully independent and responsible for self.	Transition to greater sense of independence with more responsibility for self.	In what ways am I ready to take responsibility for my life? In what ways am I ready to commit to others?
Feeling that anything is possible.	Make decisions about life's path, choosing from many possibilities that present themselves.	What kind of life do I wish to have? What kind of person do I wish to be?

*Note. From *Emerging Adulthood: The Winding Road from the Late Teens through the Twenties* (p. 8), by J. J. Arnett, 2004, New York: Oxford University Press. Copyright 2004 by Oxford University Press. Reprinted with permission.

Emerging Adults: Why Mindfulness Helps

This search for wisdom is one of the key areas in which emerging adult development and mindfulness practices converge. Mindfulness is often referred to as a *wisdom* practice because wisdom and self-understanding inevitably begin to grow when we start to pay attention to the moment-to-moment movements of our minds. As this wisdom grows, individuals often find that they develop clarity about their authentic wishes, needs, and values. A commonly used metaphor in mindfulness teachings compares the mind to a choppy, cloudy pond. As we apply awareness, the pond stills and then clears, allowing us to see what lies deep below the surface.

Emerging adults tend to have especially choppy, cloudy ponds. Looking at the tasks and goals described in Table 2.1, it is easy to see why. This developmental phase is all about not knowing what is next in any sphere of life. Questions about what type of career to follow and whom to choose as a life partner are major concerns at this stage. Underneath these questions are struggles about values and meaning. Arnett's data show that this generation of emerging adults demands meaning from their experiences; these young people expect their careers to be more than just a way to make money. Yet, at the same time, they are quite confused. They are pulled in many different directions by their parents, their peers, the media, and countless other sources. Many of them will say that they have no idea what lies ahead for them, and some find all the uncertainty terrifying. It is in this context of inquiry and confusion that mindfulness can be so useful.

Although some emerging adults thrive on the rapid pace of change and the sense of endless opportunities, others find that the uncertainty in their lives can lead to intense feelings of stress, worry, and even anxiety. The current generation of college students seems particularly plagued by negative emotions. These painful feelings can be seen in reports from the popular press about students dealing with high rates of depression and anxiety. For example, Tamar Levin reported in the *New York Times* in January 2011 that American college students' emotional health continues to decline (Levin, 2011). She reviewed the results of an annual survey showing that their emotional health had fallen to the lowest level measured since the survey began 25 years ago. More students were rating their own emotional health as relatively low. At the same time, the survey indicated that students' expectations of themselves continued to rise, with freshmen in 2010 showing record high levels of the "drive to succeed." Twenty-nine percent reported that they had frequently felt overwhelmed during their senior year in high school. This combination of feeling increased pressure to succeed while feeling less emotionally resilient can lead emerging adults to feel overwhelmed and lost, uncertain of how to deal with the competing pressures in their lives.

These struggles can be glimpsed in the goals stated by students beginning Koru, our mindfulness and meditation course. During the first class, as part of getting to know the students and building motivation for the work ahead, we ask them to share briefly something about what they are hoping to learn or gain from the class. Jesse, a 21-year-old senior, articulated the most frequently stated goal of our class participants when she said, "I just feel so stressed out all the time. I'm a senior now, and I have no idea what I'll be doing next year. I've got all this work to do, and I feel like I don't have any time. I just want to learn how to relax better."

In our experience, these struggles are multicultural phenomena. We see students from a wide range of countries, cultures, and ethnicities coming to our class and expressing these same concerns. Arnett (2004) observes that emerging adulthood occurs primarily in industrialized countries and within a cultural context influenced more by social class than ethnicity; the opportunity to delay assuming adult responsibilities is more likely to occur for individuals who have some economic freedom, regardless of ethnicity or race. That said, within the university community we see many students who are struggling to deal with severe financial constraints, but these students for the most part still fit within the developmental paradigm of emerging adulthood.

Given the characteristics of this age group and the stress and pressure that many of these young people feel, the value of developing the skills of mindfulness and meditation is readily apparent. Mindfulness and meditation, perhaps more than any other strategies or skills, are especially suited for promoting the growth and change emerging adults are experiencing. Mindfulness-based stress-management skills allow the students to quiet their anxiety and decrease their distress. Meditation practice teaches the skill of present-moment awareness, which leads to greater focus, clarity, and authenticity. These qualities, in turn, help emerging adults proceed through this important developmental stage with greater confidence. Armed with self-knowledge and peace of mind, they can deal with the challenges and choices that await them.

Having now looked at the rationale for teaching mindfulness to emerging adults, it is time to turn our attention to some specific strategies for working with this group. In the next chapter, we will look at the techniques we have found effective for engaging our students in the study and practice of mindfulness.

Strategies for Bringing Mindfulness to Emerging Adults

Emerging adults may benefit from training in mindfulness, but they don't always take to it easily. Often students are enthusiastic about the idea of learning mindfulness but then have a hard time developing the skills in a meaningful way. In fact, mindfulness is tricky for anybody to learn. It is difficult to develop the ability to watch the movement of your mind with acceptance and patience. Similarly, it is difficult to find a method for teaching emerging adults these valuable skills.

As it turns out, there's a knack to getting emerging adults to stick with meditation. In our experience, traditional methods of teaching mindfulness and meditation don't engage students long enough for them to experience the benefits. These benefits, which include decreased feelings of pressure and stress, improved focus, increases in positive emotions and greater self-knowledge, typically inspire students to forge ahead with their practice. The trick is finding a way to keep them engaged during the initial stage, when the practice can seem confusing and even frustrating at times. After considerable trial and error, we developed a model based on our understanding of what motivates students to learn and what impedes their progress. Embedded in the model are a number of strategies that we have found to be effective in capturing and holding the interest of our students.

On the following pages, we will explore these strategies. Although there is a fair amount of overlap, they can be divided roughly into three groups: strategies related to the organization and structure of the class; strategies related to general teaching techniques; and strategies for dealing with typical student reactions. We do not pretend that this is a complete list of learning techniques for this age group, but these are the ones that have worked well for our students and us and will likely also work well for you.

CHAPTER 3: KEY POINTS

- Emerging adults utilize mindfulness and meditation effectively if it is offered to them in ways that fit their developmental stage.
- You can use particular strategies to enhance learning when creating a class for teaching mindfulness to this age group.
- Organizational factors to attend to include recruiting a diverse group of students and making attendance and practice mandatory.
- Teachers must work hard to maintain the motivation of the group.
- Students learn best when you use their questions to prompt teaching with stories and metaphors.
- Emerging adults bring unique perspectives to the group that teachers can work with to facilitate learning.

Organizational Factors That Assist Learning

Certain factors related to the structure and organization of the group seem to be crucial for an effective learning environment. Creating a diverse group of participants who consistently attend the class seems necessary for a rich learning environment. Developing and communicating clear requirements for participation are also critical for the group to thrive. Here are our suggestions for managing these tasks.

A Diverse Group Leads to Richness and Depth

We have found that our classes are at their best when we have a diverse mix of students in the group; thus, we recommend that you try to gather a diverse group of young adults for your own classes. We are fortunate at Duke to have students from all over the world, representing different cultures and different points of view. We also have students from a variety of socioeconomic groups and with a diversity of sexual orientations, religious beliefs, ethnic groups, and regions in the United States. In addition, we have students who are undergraduates, graduate students, and professional students; thus, a wide range of emerging adults is represented. This range of diversity may not be available in your pool of potential students, but we encourage you to seek students who can bring a variety of perspectives to your group. We find that a high degree of diversity enhances mindfulness training in a few key ways.

Learning to identify the internal judgments we make is an important first step in mindfulness training. Sometimes we see those judgments more clearly when we are faced with others who differ from us in some way that seems important to us. Second, acceptance evolves as judgments are released. As students from diverse backgrounds see each other having identical struggles with present-moment awareness, they see similarities rather than differences. Judgments are then naturally released. Third, the richness of the stories and the explorations of the group are influenced by the degree of diversity present. For example, in one class, a student from Thailand who had been raised as a Buddhist and had come to the United States to study biochemistry shared a story about the pressures he was facing as he adjusted to the university community. An African American woman from the southern United States who was studying at the divinity school was able to identify with his struggles and offered some wisdom from her own experience. Everyone in the group, including the teachers, benefits from these sorts of exchanges.

Because a multicultural environment is important to the function of the group, we strongly encourage prospective teachers to recruit group members in a variety of ways (see chapter 5 for suggestions on how to do this). Making an effort to advertise your mindfulness and meditation class widely will produce a more diverse group of students, which will, in turn, lead to a deeper and more complex experience for all.

Small-Group Learning with Peers Is Important

Emerging adults care about what their peers think. This is perhaps one reason that small groups in which the students have a chance to talk and listen to each other work best. In our experience, students learn meditation in a small-group setting better than when they are taught individually. Although we both work with individuals therapeutically and often teach mindfulness skills, we have found that the dynamic of the small group provides direction and motivation for learning that can not be produced in one-to-one teaching.

Scholars have examined the efficacy of different learning models, including the model called *small-group learning* (SGL). The title of one study (Gaudet, Ramer, Nakonechny, Cragg, & Ramer, 2010) mirrors our experience: "Small-Group Learning in an Upper-Level University Biology Class Enhances Academic Performance and Student Attitudes Toward Group Work." In this study, the results showed that the SGL students had significantly higher final exam grades than their peers who were learning independently. Additionally, student attitudes were more positive toward the SGL model. As noted above, these results are consistent with our experience, and support our contention that emerging adults have the best chance of learning mindfulness and meditation if the teaching occurs in the context of small-group learning.

Much of the teaching in our classes is done during the *check-in* at the beginning of each class, when each student is given the opportunity to share his or her experience in practicing mindfulness skills over the previous week. Typically at each check-in, some students feel enthused because they are making good progress in learning the skills, whereas others feel discouraged by barriers they've encountered.

As the students share their experience, we take the opportunity to teach, often linking the comments made by different students. For example, the first student may say that he's had a "good" week with meditation, and he describes feeling more relaxed and focused. The next student may say that her mind has been wandering; she has had a "bad" week and is feeling frustrated. The teachers can then ask the group (while taking the opportunity to comment on the judgments about a "good week" versus a "bad week") if anyone else has had the same experience. Usually there will be another student who can then share his or her experience and enlarge the discussion. Looking for ideas and solutions from other students is an effective way to help problem-solve and build motivation.

When the students see that their peers share some of their struggles, they feel more connected and less hopeless about the process; when they hear their peers relating improvements and successes, their motivation increases. The dynamic around these peer interactions is one of the driving forces behind a successful class.

Participation and Practice Are Not Optional

We have found that creating a structure with strict boundaries and clear expectations is crucial for this age group. Students are conditioned to be externally motivated when it comes to learning new information or skills. This means that if you want to teach them something new that can be difficult to learn, initially you have to require them to do the work. Once they have had sufficient experience with mindfulness and meditation, they will probably notice some compelling changes that will keep them interested. For many students, just a few weeks of required practice will help them cross this threshold.

Students have basically always been students. This may seem obvious, but what it comes down to is that their job has been to learn, for the most part, what others feel they need to learn. It's just life as they know it. Even in college, when they are allowed to select their classes, they still have to read the books the professor chooses and complete the homework that they are assigned. This is the routine they know and are comfortable with, though they complain about it and resent it at times.

Students have very busy schedules, and they tend to complete tasks based on deadlines. "The math problems are due in the morning. I'll get started on them at midnight." "The paper is due at 5 p.m. tomorrow. I'll start on it when I get up in the morning." Not every student procrastinates to this degree, of course, but they are truly extremely busy. There are so many tasks they have to do that the optional ones often don't get done, even if (especially if?) students know that it would be "good for them." So, we have discovered that the course works best if mindfulness practice is one of those things they have to do. Therefore, when they sign up for the course, they are told that attendance at all four classes is required. If they can't clear their schedules and guarantee that they will be at each class, they may not enroll in the course. Similarly, daily meditation and mindfulness skills practice is required homework. We emphasize that it is not optional. The students are given a log for their daily practice, and it must be returned to the teachers each week. We don't actually grade the logs, but the students fill them out and return them quite diligently, seemingly responding to our clear statement that it is an absolute requirement.

They also have a required text for the course. We don't have a lot of time in class to discuss the text, but we ask them to bring quotations from the book and they generally comply.

Of course, you have to communicate all of these requirements to the students with humor and warmth or they are unlikely to proceed; but they are used to getting home-work and know how to respond. It is effective to capitalize on this nice bit of condition-ing. This approach also selects for the students who are most motivated to learn, the ones who are willing to make a commitment. Because an essential part of the learning is the small-group format, a fairly high level of motivation throughout the group is important for the group dynamic.

Making attendance and homework mandatory is a departure from the way mind-fulness and meditation are usually taught, and we were initially reluctant to make this change. Perhaps surprisingly, the students responded to the increased structure by dem-onstrating dramatically increased enthusiasm for the class. This seems paradoxical, but, of course, everything about mindfulness is. If you require the students to practice, they will. If they practice, they will fairly quickly start to feel the benefits. Once they experi-ence positive change, their internal motivation to continue begins to develop. Also, man-datory attendance allows the group process to thrive; it's not possible to create a cohesive learning group if only some students show up for each class. By the end of the class, we expect the students to be internally motivated to keep practicing mindfulness skills and meditation. But you have to start somewhere, and we've learned that it is critical to create a structure that externally motivates emerging adults if you expect them to get off to a good start.

Teaching Strategies That Assist Learning

The next two strategies address general approaches to teaching mindfulness and medita-tion that we have employed in our model. Both of these strategies reflect our understand-ing of emerging adults as well as our experience with our students.

Maintaining Motivation Is Absolutely Necessary

Teachers must attend constantly to the motivation level of the students or the class won't get off the ground. This age group is reinforced by progress and improvement, and students tend to make rapid judgments about what is worth doing. This means that from the begin-ning you have to be very active, identifying progress and helping to translate it into practi-cal gains. Similarly, obstacles to progress need to be assessed and surmounted before the students judge the course to be a waste of time. This active approach differs from the more traditional methods of teaching mindfulness and meditation, which rely to some degree on the solutions and answers unfolding over time. With emerging adults, their impatience for improvement and change forces the teacher to use a much more engaged approach.

For example, in the first class, the students learn a skill called *dynamic breathing*. It's a ridiculous-looking but highly effective breathing technique for managing stress and anxiety that involves flapping the arms and bouncing the knees while breathing rapidly through the nose. The students laugh with embarrassment as we teach the skill and sometimes express doubt about its usefulness. However, after a week of being required to practice it, they often find it very helpful. When we introduce the skill, we laugh and joke about how silly it seems and then suggest some situations in which it might be useful. "Next time it's 3 a.m. and you are trying to finish the paper that's due at 8 a.m., and you're so tired and stressed that you can't think, get up and spend 2 minutes doing dynamic breathing. I promise that your head will be clear after that."

Sharing the successes of former students can also help. Sometimes we tell them about the student who said that dynamic breathing was working much better for her than her former strategy: lots of caffeine. She found that dynamic breathing kept her awake and alert while she finished her work, and then she could easily get to sleep once the work was done. "If I drink enough coffee to keep myself awake, then I can't get to sleep once I'm finally done with my work. I really like the breathing because it keeps me awake, but only as long as I want to be awake." We also sometimes mention the student who told the class, quite hilariously, how she would go into a bathroom stall in the library late at night and do "chicken breathing," the students' often used nickname for dynamic breathing. She said it worked very well when she felt so worried about getting her work done that she couldn't think clearly. "Every time I get stuck, I just run into the bathroom and do chicken breathing. It works great and it also makes me laugh."

Removing obstacles is similarly important. If during check-in a student expresses discouragement about his or her practice during the previous week, you can try to identify what is getting in the way and attempt to solve the problem. For example, a very common complaint from students is that they fall asleep every time they try to meditate. When you hear this, you can empathize about how tired they must be and then move on to the task of helping them find ways around this obstacle. Do they feel tired all the time? Probably they are not getting enough sleep in general, but they don't feel they have enough time to sleep more (see "Feeling Pressed for Time" below). Where are they trying to meditate? "Lying in bed," a frequent reply, will almost always lead to sleep in a sleep-deprived student. Look for ideas about other times and places to meditate. Also, suggest that the students focus on the more active meditation skills, like dynamic breathing or walking meditation. Sharing an example of a student who has found a good solution also helps. Sometimes we describe the student who at first found that the only form of meditation she could do and stay awake was dynamic breathing, but as she continued to practice, she eventually was able to stay awake during sitting meditations.

Another frequently cited obstacle is the opposite of the sleepiness problem: extreme restlessness. Chandra expressed a common problem when she said that her mind was so restless and wandered so much that she thought she was someone who just couldn't meditate. A good place to begin when you hear this concern is by addressing the incorrect belief that someone might be constitutionally unable to meditate. We like to help the students distinguish between what is "hard" versus what is "impossible". They are often surprised that it is hard to sit still and focus their minds, so they quickly jump to the assumption that it is impossible.

Students respond well to being reminded that they obviously can do hard tasks, or they never would have made it into college in the first place. Most students are familiar with the idea that they have to train their bodies if they want to accomplish a hard task like running a marathon; it makes sense to them that if they work out, they can run faster or lift heavier weights. For this reason, it is helpful to use an analogy between body training and mind training. You can try saying something like this:

> If I asked you to bench press 200 pounds, you probably wouldn't be able to do it, but you would immediately know that there is a strategy for getting to the point where you can lift heavy weights. You probably wouldn't assume that it is not possible for you to lift heavy weights. You would immediately know that to lift a heavy weight, you have to start practicing with lighter weights and eventually work your way up to the heavier ones. It's exactly the same with training your mind. The "200-pound weight" of mindfulness practice is that moment when you are so anxious or angry that you feel overwhelmed by your feelings. It takes a lot of mind training to work your way up to lifting that kind of emotional weight. That's why we begin with 10 minutes a day in relatively calm situations. As you practice with these "lighter weights" you gradually get better and better at focusing your mind, paying attention to your thoughts and feelings and accepting them as they are as you let go of all judgments; your mindfulness "muscle" gets stronger. You become more able to respond skillfully to a stressful situation rather than just react automatically.

After sharing this analogy, you could go back to Chandra and suggest that she start her mind training with a very light weight. What about trying to sit quietly and count 10 breaths? If she does that 10 times during the day (setting her phone to remind her), she'll have completed her mindfulness homework for the day. Gradually, she should find that she can sit for longer periods, working her way up to at least 10 minutes at a time.

By problem-solving, using metaphors and analogies, and sharing examples of what has worked for other students, the teacher illuminates the concrete benefits of mindfulness practice and leads the students around any obstacles they encounter. This, in turn, leads to more motivation; and as we said earlier, maintaining motivation is absolutely necessary.

Stories, Not Lectures, Keep Them Engaged

Using stories as learning tools is one way in which our model adheres to more traditional methods for teaching meditation. Throughout history, metaphors, stories, and parables have been the bedrock of teaching in the meditative traditions. Anyone who has spent time learning and practicing meditation will have heard the same stories, or variations of the stories, that we use when we teach. Our stories are not new, but they are the ones that we find useful in teaching emerging adults. At the same time, any number of stories and metaphors are likely to be useful, and you are encouraged to try out your favorite ones. What's important here is to avoid lecturing to the students. Sharing stories and telling tales is the best way to hold their attention and illustrate for them the complexities and paradoxes of mindfulness.

Two of the metaphors we use have already been described. Above, we discussed building the "mindfulness muscle" by practicing with light emotional weights. In chapter 2, we talked about clearing the choppy ponds of our busy minds. Because students often express frustration with the busy-ness of their minds, we have other metaphors that we regularly use in addressing this problem. For example, we talk about the thoughts moving through the mind like a rushing, roaring river. The river is always moving, and the thoughts are always rushing along. Mindfulness is the skill that allows the student to sit on the bank and watch the thoughts rather than be in the river, carried away by the thoughts. We often say:

> At first, you'll find that you climb onto the bank and then fall right back into the river. Climb onto the bank, fall back into the river, over and over. Practicing mindfulness of your thoughts is actually just being willing to climb out of the river, over and over. Every time you turn your attention to the present moment and notice what you are thinking, you have just climbed out of the river. "Staying on the bank" is noticing the next thought instead of getting caught up in the story of the first one. If you stick with the process, you will eventually notice that you start to sit on the bank a bit longer, and the river may actually begin to slow down. As this starts to happen, you'll really get a feel for the difference between sitting on the bank and watching the thoughts go by versus being in the middle of the river, washed away by the thoughts.

Another useful metaphor illustrates the difference between *observing mind* and *thinking mind* by comparing thinking mind to a hyperactive puppy. Thinking mind is what our mind is doing most of the time: planning, comparing, judging, making decisions, or worrying. Observing mind kicks in when we begin to develop awareness of our thoughts and feelings as they arise. Observing mind is curious and relaxed, helping us to develop a broader perspective on our mental activity. With mindfulness, we are cultivating and strengthening observing mind while quieting thinking mind. To help students better understand these two states of mind, thinking mind can be characterized as a busy puppy that is always running around, bouncing off the walls, jumping from one activity to the next. Observing mind doesn't have a chance to gain some control until thinking mind settles down a bit.

This metaphor often comes up when we are teaching the students to use *gathas*. Gathas are short mindfulness poems; their use is explained more fully in chapter 7.

Essentially, they are tools that can be used to help anchor the attention in the present moment. When you use a gatha, it's like tossing your puppy, your thinking mind, a bone. The puppy settles down, stays in one place for a bit, and gnaws on the bone, anchoring your thoughts in the present moment, allowing observing mind to flourish.

As we noted previously, stories about other students' experiences can be very engaging. Stories from the teacher's life can also be helpful. Here's one that we sometimes use to illustrate the way our thoughts can influence our mood and create unnecessary stress:

> Often, at the end of the day, I'm faced with cleaning the kitchen and doing the dishes before I can go to bed. Now, I've got a busy life. I work, I've got a small child to care for, a house to maintain, a big dog that needs walking, countless other chores, and usually by the end of the day, I'm pretty tired. But still, the dishes have to be done. If I pay attention, I'll notice that I'm having thoughts like "Why do I have to do the dishes? It's not fair. I always do the dishes. [This is false, by the way. My husband does them far more often than me, but when I'm grumpy and enjoying a little self-pity, often my thoughts aren't so picky about the truth.] I have to do everything around here. I'm too tired, and I hate doing this anyway." You can imagine what this does to my mood: I end up very grumpy and irritable. If I notice these thoughts and make a choice to become mindful, that is, to shift my attention to the sensations of my present-moment experience, then the scene changes dramatically. Instead of being lost in negative thoughts, I notice the pleasant feel of the warm water, the smell of the bubbles, the satisfying clink of the dishes as they go into the dishwasher, the movement of my arm as I wipe down the counters. I might hum a soothing melody to myself to keep my thinking mind a little quiet. I discover that, actually, washing dishes is not hard or even unpleasant when I stay present and pay attention. The task gets done regardless, but how I feel while I'm doing it and when I'm finished is vastly different if I do the task mindfully.

Even though the students don't necessarily have exactly the same issue in their lives, they can still relate to the unpleasant feelings that arise when we are doing something we dislike. Dishwashing is an act commonly used by meditation teachers to demonstrate the way mindfulness can change our perceptions; this personal example helps students see that shifting their attention to the present moment can give them relief from negative thought patterns that affect their mood.

Characteristic Student Attitudes and Strategies for Working with Them

Our last set of strategies has been developed in response to specific attitudes and perspectives that we hear repeatedly from our students. Below, we will describe these characteristic attitudes and share our ideas for working with them.

Skeptical but Open to Change

"Overall, a really helpful experience and unexpectedly so." This quote was taken from a student evaluation at the end of one of our classes. It captures perfectly the skepticism and openness that are so wonderfully intermingled in emerging adults. The students often bring to the class a fair amount of doubt about this whole meditation business. They are easily put off by anything that's too "new-agey" or "touchy-feely." They're ready to reject new ideas if they are too weird or too different from their own culture. But at the same time, they are very flexible about suspending their doubts in the interest of trying something new. Because emerging adults are so open to exploration, they are rarely completely stuck in their own ways. They are surprisingly willing to try out new ideas, even when they are skeptical. Working with this combination of skepticism and openness requires careful attention to language, making sure that students can relate to the examples and stories used in the class.

One way we work with the students' skepticism is to spend a little time reviewing some of the scientific research on the benefits of mindfulness and meditation. Students tend to have an academic orientation. They will often be reassured to learn that scientists have spent a fair amount of time asking the same questions they are asking and have found some clear benefits of investing time in mindfulness practice. Often the opportunity to talk a little about the science behind the work will arise in response to a student's question. For example, one of our graduate students, Ashok, asked if there was any evidence that meditation could help him feel calmer. This gave us the opportunity to talk with him about some of the studies that show decreased levels of stress in subjects who have practiced meditation. In chapter 4 we review some of the mindfulness and meditation research that may be most salient to your emerging adults. You will find that a basic knowledge of this information is helpful in addressing students' skepticism when it arises.

Another useful way for teachers to address skepticism is to describe their own experiences. Anyone who tries to learn the rather difficult and sometimes boring practice of mindfulness meditation is going to have some doubts. We have found that sharing our own experiences of both doubt and progress provides a model for the students when they have similar challenges. For example, Holly likes to recount her own struggles with restlessness and doubt by relating the following story:

> When I first started trying to meditate, it was very hard for me to sit still. I felt so restless. I remember the first time I attended a meditation group. I was shocked when I learned that we were all going to sit in silent meditation for 30 minutes, take a short break, and then sit for another 30 minutes. An hour of meditation! That seemed impossible to me. I couldn't believe the other people in the group seemed to think this was a good idea. I remember feeling like time was going so slowly, that the person in charge of the clock had certainly fallen asleep, and that

I was being tortured and it was all a big waste of time. I started making judgments about the other meditators, wondering if they were all deranged! But I remembered the admonitions to reserve judgment, be patient, and see for myself, and I managed to stick with it, even returning to that same group. Before long, it became clear to me that things were starting to change. I was feeling more peaceful, and my life was getting easier as I learned to release my judgments and focus my attention on the present moment. After a while, the positive changes I was experiencing in my own life became my source of motivation for continued practice, and here I am, years later, still practicing and still feeling the transformation that it is has wrought for me. Believe it or not, I still go to that same meditation group! Your experience, of course, may be different, but we invite you to reserve judgment, be patient, and see what happens as you devote yourself for the next few weeks to the daily practice of mindfulness.

Finally, one of the most effective methods for dealing with skepticism is to address it directly, by noting it, and then invite the students to stay curious, keep their minds open, and see what happens. For example, when you introduce dynamic breathing or the gathas (both discussed above), some students may express some skepticism. We recommend acknowledging that these practices do sound a little strange but that other students have found them helpful. Then encourage the students to keep an open mind as they try them. Remember, mindfulness is all about staying present, with an attitude of curiosity toward whatever the present moment brings.

Not So Accepting of Acceptance

There are important aspects of mindfulness that must be communicated to the students: acceptance, nonstriving, nonjudging and patience, to name a few. Students resist a little when they are first introduced to these ideas. The idea of accepting things as they are is particularly uncomfortable to persons in this age group. Remember, this is the age of exploration, striving, seeking, and change; telling emerging adults that the best way to manage their stressful challenges is to sit quietly and do nothing can drive them crazy. In addition, teaching non-doing may make them think at first that you are crazy. This brings us to one of the first paradoxes that we have to address in mindfulness training: the first goal is to let go of all goals. So, although we acknowledge that academic excellence, for example, is an important goal, achieving that goal involves letting go of the idea of being the perfect student. Instead, we teach the students to stay present, attend to their work as best they can, and see what emerges. Students don't usually take to this concept at first. Eventually, with great perseverance on your part, the students will come to appreciate this paradox is an important piece of the beauty and brilliance of mindfulness.

Here is another paradox, or actually the same paradox, just stated a little differently: nonstriving is the only way to get what you want. When we are anxious or feel unhappy, we believe with all our hearts that if we could only change x, y, and z, we would be happy. Mindfulness theory and practice teach us the opposite: we will only achieve happiness when we stop feeling attached to the idea that x, y, and z need to change.

In mindfulness parlance, this is known as *acceptance*. Students resist the idea of acceptance when they first hear about it and will often argue about its validity. One articulate and persuasive young man pointed out that the Nazis would have taken over the world if everyone had practiced acceptance. Of course, if the Nazis had been practicing acceptance, they wouldn't have felt compelled to pursue genocide and world domination. That point aside, when students react against the idea of acceptance, it is usually because they are confusing it with what Eckhart Tolle refers to in his best-selling book, *The Power of Now* (Tolle, 1999), as *passive resignation*, a state of indifference and hopelessness that is very uncomfortable to them. It is important to be well armed with stories and examples of acceptance that clearly differentiate true acceptance from passive resignation, because you won't get anywhere with emerging adults until they are clear on this point. The text for the class is useful for this purpose; Kabat-Zinn's (1994) book is filled with inspirational and clear teaching about acceptance.

Acceptance is a very active state. Acceptance is not the thought, "Oh, well, there's nothing I can do about it. I'll just have to accept things the way they are." Acceptance is the thought, "Let me look deeply into this situation so that I understand the reality of it. From this place of clear-seeing, I can then choose with wisdom the best action for me to take." Acceptance is the state of actively opening to the truth in the present moment. This act of seeing the truth of this moment is what leads to right action in the next moment.

To convey this to the students, we suggest using examples from their academic or social life. Students can identify with being in a hopeless situation with regard to completing a project or assignment on time, so this can be a good topic to use to illustrate the difference between acceptance and passive resignation.

We might say the following to the students:

Let's say it is 3 a.m. and you still have 10 more pages to write of your 12-page paper that is due at 8 a.m. You've been working on it for hours and are completely stuck. For some reason, this particular paper is not coming together, and you have waited until the final hour to start working on it. In this situation, what would passive resignation look like? Starting to panic or cry, or perhaps binge drinking, not finishing the paper, and not doing anything else proactive. Denial, the completely nonmindful approach, might lead you to stay up working relentlessly until the deadline passed, leaving you exhausted and without a plan B.

If you were staying mindful and practicing acceptance, sometime around 3 a.m. you would clearly see the truth: that you were completely exhausted and not working effectively. You would see the emotions of fear, anger, and frustration arising, and you would understand them as unpleasant but normal reactions to being stuck in a truly aversive situation. You would recognize that you started the paper too late, but this recognition would be free of harsh judgment. You would just see, without judging, that it does indeed take you more than 12 hours to research and write a paper of this size: useful information for the next project. You would understand that it is no longer possible to produce a good-quality paper by the deadline. With this clear understanding, you could then choose appropriate action, considering various options. Perhaps turning in a very poor paper and getting a poor grade is better than submitting no paper at all. Perhaps sending an apologetic e-mail to your professor, promising to get the paper in as soon as possible, is a good solution. Perhaps asking to meet with your professor in person is an even better solution. Perhaps getting some sleep so that you can think more clearly about how to handle this situation in the morning is the best solution. Developing these alternatives and choosing wisely among them is not possible until you accept that your Plan A, having a brilliant paper ready by the deadline, is not happening.

The social life of emerging adults is often a source of painful feelings that require some acceptance. Here's an example that students can often identify with:

You have a tremendous crush on your best friend's girlfriend, and she doesn't know you exist. In passive resignation mode, you spend endless months secretly suffering from the pain of unrequited love, never making attempts at more realistic romantic attachments and perhaps letting the situation poison your relationship with your friend. In acceptance mode, you acknowledge without judgment the way it feels to be in love with someone who doesn't share your feelings; it's a pretty miserable feeling, but it is what it is. You see truly what your chances and choices are, and act in a way that is likely to create the least suffering for all. Only if you really recognize all the important variables in this situation, including your own values, can you act with wisdom.

Mindfulness practice shows us that we suffer when our thoughts and behaviors are focused on trying to achieve a certain outcome or believing we need things to be a certain way. Mindfulness teaches that, paradoxically, we can only create the kind of change we seek in our life when we develop acceptance of how things are right now. For students, often the change they want is to be finished with whatever task is creating stress at the moment. They frequently say that they will be happy as soon as they finish this paper—or this class, or this semester, or this year, or this degree program. This type of thinking, which pushes happiness into the future, is common, but emerging adults seem particularly drawn to it.

You can teach the students that a more mindful approach to developing less stress and more happiness in life is to simply shift their attention to the present moment. Instead of fantasizing about how good things will be in the future, they should bring their attention fully into the present moment. Boris shared his experience when he started putting this into action. He said, "I always feel so restless in math class that I can hardly stand to sit there. I spend the whole time just waiting for the class to be over and thinking about what I'll do when I get out of there. So, this week, I switched to just really paying attention to what was going on in the class. Focusing on what the professor was saying and being open to what was going on in the class completely changed my experience. The class seemed to be over in no time, and I actually enjoyed it." Boris is demonstrating what happened when he went from making the judgment that he could only be happy when his class was over to *accepting* that he would be in the class for a defined period of time. Once he developed this acceptance, he became willing to see what would happen if he shifted his attention from the future to the present moment. He discovered that his impatience and restlessness in class were not due to the class itself, but rather to his mind's persistent pull away from his present-moment experience. (See the "Frequently Asked Questions" at the end of chapter 6 for more ideas on working with the concept of acceptance.)

Feeling Pressed for Time

Students constantly tell us that they don't have time to meditate. Their sense of a lack of time may be the biggest barrier to maintaining their commitment to do their mindfulness homework. They perceive themselves as being pushed to the limit by a multitude of competing responsibilities. The idea of making time for one more task seems absurd, if not completely impossible. Yet, they have signed up and shown up for this class because they know that what they have been doing is not working for them. They are willing to try to make the time for something new, but at the same time, they can't imagine how they will do that.

Students are masters of technology and adept at multitasking. Research on attention and multitasking shows that the brain doesn't focus attention on more than one thing at a time; instead, it rapidly shifts attention between tasks (Ophir, Nass, & Wagner, 2009). Rather than increasing efficiency, these rapid shifts in attention can decrease efficiency (Marois, 2006). Worse for students, multitasking can actually impede the learning process. Students haven't gotten this message at all. They have the misimpression that multitasking is the only answer to their perceived shortage of time, and they have usually tried to deal with the problem by switching their attention at an increasingly frenetic pace from one idea or task to the next.

Mindfulness is anti-multitasking. By teaching mindfulness, we are trying to break the students' addiction to multitasking. Mindfulness is about steadying your attention, holding it constant, observing without judging or trying to change each moment as it arises. Surprisingly, when you start to pay attention, the perception of how much time you have begins to change.

Expressing her trouble with finding time to meditate, Manuela said, "I really mean to do my meditation practice each day, but I keep running out of time. I mean, I literally have no time. I hardly even go out with my friends anymore, and I just feel pressured all the time. I know it sounds stupid, but I can't seem to make those 10 minutes a day happen." In helping students find the time to meditate, we tend to use two approaches at the same time: a practical approach similar to the one we use to address any other obstacle and a philosophical approach to challenge the way they think about the time that they have.

In using the practical approach, you could work with Manuela's time pressure in the same way you work with other obstacles encountered by students. Start by expressing empathy about how busy and pressured her life feels. Then problem-solve and help her look for some of the natural spaces in her day, patches of time that may go unnoticed or feel otherwise wasted. Ask her: "How do you get to school each day?" "What time do you get up?" "How much time is there between your classes?" "Are there a few minutes in the middle of the day that you can use to meditate?" "What about right before you go to sleep?" Often these kinds of questions help the students formulate a strategy for finding those extra 10 minutes.

In addition to addressing some of these practical problems, we like to question students about what time means to them. Students tend to respond well to these philosophical discussions about time. For example you might ask, "What does it mean that you don't have enough time? You've got the time that you've got—the same time that we've all got. The real question is, how do you want to spend it—worrying and feeling stressed or breathing mindfully while you sit on the quad between classes?" Ask the students to try to notice if the way they think about time and the tasks they must accomplish affects how they feel about the time that they have.

Sometimes we tell the story about our student, Matt, who discovered, after a period of feeling that he didn't have time to meditate, that he actually spent a lot of his time waiting: waiting for class to start, waiting for friends to meet him, waiting in line at the store, waiting for the light to turn green, even waiting for a class to end. He noticed that if he thought of this time as "waiting," he felt impatient, as though his time was being wasted. He became very curious about the difference between waiting for something to happen or change and just observing what was happening or changing. He discovered that if he perceived his waiting times as opportunities to get his meditation homework done, he could really relax into these free minutes, using the time to practice mindfulness. By making this simple shift in perception, his experience of time pressure changed dramatically. This is often the first step toward finding the time to regularly practice mindfulness.

In talking about waiting, Margaret likes to tell her own story of how to manage waiting in airports and on long flights or even on buses or trains. Our students travel often— back and forth to home, to programs in other countries, and so on. Here's what Margaret says:

> How many of you have had to sit at gates or on planes for long periods of time and felt frustrated and impatient? Well, what a wonderful opportunity for practicing mindfulness! [Students almost always laugh.] I travel a lot and, having lived in different countries, have spent hundreds of hours waiting in various airports.

When I finally learned about mindfulness, I began to use those hours for practice. Now, when I'm sitting in the airport, I often simply close my eyes and practice belly breathing. When I am on a long flight, I never look at my watch but spend much of the time meditating. And I've discovered how much quicker and more pleasant the flights have become!

Eager to Feel Less Anxious

Anxiety, stress, tension, and worry are the demons that most frequently bring students to our classes. Over and over, students tell us that they are coming to the class primarily because they feel overwhelmed by anxiety and stress. They report that because of their high anxiety level, they are having trouble sleeping, concentrating, completing important tasks, and feeling a sense of pleasure. Their level of distress is fairly high, and they are seeking relief. Learning acceptance of the stress in their lives involves helping the students develop mindfulness skills that allow them to tolerate and work with their feelings.

Often, by the time they get to the class, the students have tried unsuccessfully to find some way of calming themselves. They may be at the point of feeling that they just can't take it anymore and need some rapid relief. For this reason, the first class is designed to give the students tools that can directly address their high level of anxiety.

In the first class, you will teach two breathing exercises: belly breathing, an exercise for activating the parasympathetic nervous system (more about that in chapter 4) and thus calming the body, and dynamic breathing, an exercise for clearing the mind and releasing high levels of anxiety and tension. The class closes with a guided body scan. After practicing the two breathing exercises and being guided through the body scan, the students generally leave the class feeling significantly calmer than when they entered. This is yet another way to shore up motivation, but mostly it just honors the importance of helping them feel better. The students are often suffering when they enter that first class, and it is necessary to recognize and address their suffering.

Students' anxiety is often expressed as constant worry and rumination. Their minds travel in obsessive circles as they think about past mistakes or feared future events. Their level of stress and physical discomfort increases the more their minds spin. Mindfulness meditation is particularly well suited to help students break these ruminative thought patterns. As you teach them to meditate, you teach them to release worries, focusing their minds instead on their present-moment experience. Each of the guided meditations you will take the students through is designed to help them focus and calm their minds. These guided meditations are described in detail in chapters 6 to 9, which are devoted to the specifics of each class. Another mindfulness skill you will teach, guided imagery, also helps students focus their minds and calm their anxiety; this skill is discussed in chapter 8.

The students are not the only ones with goals for the class; as teachers, we often articulate the goal of helping the students to find greater contentment and joy in their lives. Calming their anxiety is an important first step toward achieving that goal.

Now that we have reviewed the theory and strategies that we have used in developing our model, let us turn our attention to the science behind the work. Research on the benefits of stress management in general, and mindfulness in particular, is abundant. A fair amount of it is specifically focused on the emerging adult population. The next chapter reviews this research and its relevance to teaching mindfulness to emerging adults.

The Research Behind
Our Teaching

"Mindfulness and Health Behaviors: Is Paying Attention Good for You?" This is the interesting title of a study by Roberts and Danoff-Burg (2010). More than 500 college undergraduates participated in the study. They completed extensive questionnaires measuring their mindfulness in relation to perceived health, health behaviors, health-related activity restriction, and stress. Five aspects of mindfulness were assessed: nonreactivity, nonjudgment, observation, awareness, and describing. Among the health behaviors were smoking, exercise, overall health, and sleep quality. The measures of mindfulness were correlated to the health measures and to stress. The researchers found that mindfulness promotes mental and physical health in college students by decreasing their stress. This is just one example of the many published studies that demonstrate the benefits of practicing mindfulness for emerging adults.

The number of scientific studies investigating mindfulness has increased exponentially over the past few decades. Like the above study, a significant portion of this work has been focused on emerging adults. This chapter will explore some of this research, but please keep in mind that this is by no means a comprehensive review of the mindfulness and stress management scientific literature. We are simply dipping our toes in the water. And don't worry: you don't need a scientific background to understand the key points in this chapter.

Many of our students do have a scientific background and are eager to learn something of the science behind our model. John is a good example:

John, a sophomore biology major, tells us in the first class that he is here to learn to meditate because he hopes "it's good for me." Like so many of his fellow students, he is feeling somewhat overwhelmed by his studies, and a friend who attended the Koru course recommended it. The friend said that the course helped him deal with his stress better, which John hopes will happen for him. However, he is skeptical and, as a scientist, wonders how meditation works in the body and what the benefits really are.

CHAPTER 4: KEY POINTS

- There is abundant scientific research, much of it in emerging adult populations, that shows the benefits of training in mindfulness and meditation.
- Students find it helpful to hear about the research that describes the potential benefits of developing a mindfulness practice.
- Students are particularly interested in research that addresses the concerns that bring them to the class, such as feeling less stressed, improving their academic performance, and improving their general sense of well-being.
- Mindfulness can also be helpful for students who struggle with attention deficit disorder or eating disorders, conditions that are common in emerging adults.

Like many of the students who come to our class, John is seeking reassurance that it will be worth the sacrifice of his time and energy to learn the skills we wish to teach him. He may ask questions about some of the physiological effects of mindfulness and stress management training. It will be helpful for him to hear about the scientific evidence that validates the benefits of spending time developing the habit of mindfulness.

This chapter is meant to prepare you for students like John. We believe that it will be helpful for you to be familiar with some of this basic research. Many of the opportunities for teaching arise spontaneously in response to students' questions; having good knowledge of the science behind the skills will allow you to make the most of these teachable moments. There is solid scientific research buttressing everything you will teach. Research in mind–body medicine, meditation, stress, and psychoneuroimmunology supports our practices with scientific evidence.

Throughout the classes we inject small bits of this science into our lessons to add an additional dimension to the learning and to respect the students' academic orientation. On occasion, students ask for copies of relevant scientific studies on mindfulness, and you may decide at times to provide them. However, it is important to keep in mind that our students do not (in most cases) come to us for didactic scientific presentations. They come for relief—relief from stress, anxiety, and the highly competitive college culture. They want to learn how to calm themselves and how to cope with stress. Many are eager to learn some form of meditation.

This chapter reviews some of the basic physiology related to stress and relaxation and provides examples of the research on mindfulness and meditation. We hope that it will allow you to become familiar with some of the scientific research addressing the personal goals that tend to be most important to emerging-adult students. Finally, you will see what research shows regarding the benefits of mindfulness for two challenges that our emerging adults sometimes face: attention deficit disorder and eating disorders.

A Quick Guide to Scientific Studies

If you are unfamiliar with the world and language of scientific research, here is a short orientation that will help you understand the rest of this chapter. If you are a research scientist, you may want to skip this section.

In perhaps the most common type of research study, the *controlled trial*, researchers first develop a hypothesis and then perform a study to test it by comparing two groups of people. An example of a hypothesis is that mindfulness meditation training helps people with stress. In this example, the researchers would want to compare and look for differences between individuals who receive mindfulness training and those who don't. The latter group is called the *control group*. The training is called the *intervention*, and the scientists would have to develop ways to measure stress before and after the intervention. In the world of psychological research, these measurements often take the form of questionnaires that the participants complete; the questionnaires are standardized and validated to reliably measure the factors that interest the researchers. In the end, what researchers are looking for are significant differences between the intervention group and the control group. *Significance* is a statistical term and thus is highly specific. In our example, the researchers will have proved their hypothesis if the intervention group has significantly lower measures of stress than the control group.

In this chapter, you will find examples of a second type of study: the *prospective cohort study*. In this kind of research, the researchers evaluate a group of people for certain medical conditions and/or lifestyle factors, such as how much exercise a person gets or how much he or she smokes; these people are then followed for several years to find out if any of the variables seen the first time contribute to the development of disease in later life. The study authors often look at *risk factors* for a disease. An example of a risk factor is smoking, which increases the risk of developing lung cancer later in life.

Yet another type of study is the *pilot study*, of which there are examples in this chapter. This is a preliminary study, often with a small number of participants, to test a theory on a small group before going to a larger group. In a pilot study, often there is no control group. Instead, a group of individuals is selected who have a symptom or disorder; they receive the intervention, and then any change is measured after the intervention. For example, the researchers might have the hypothesis that mindfulness training improves sleep quality. They would enroll participants with insomnia and measure their symptoms before the intervention (in other words, at *baseline*), provide the intervention, and then measure the symptoms afterward. Pilot studies are very useful for illuminating trends that warrant further study. Their findings are helpful and instructive, but they don't provide evidence as strong as that provided by controlled trials.

A Little Physiology—What Does Mindfulness Actually Do in the Body?

How do mindfulness meditation and stress management contribute to the physical and mental health of young adults and thus help them to lead healthier lives? In order to understand the physiology on a basic level, we recommend that you learn something about the parasympathetic nervous system (PNS), the part of our nervous system that calms us. Mindfulness and meditation skills stimulate the PNS, which is one of two main branches of the autonomic nervous system. When we consciously relax, the PNS kicks into action. It calms us and reduces our feeling of stress, as opposed to the sympathetic nervous system (SNS), which evokes the fight-or-flight response in us. These actions of the PNS powerfully influence our physical and emotional well-being. Diaphragmatic or belly breathing, a skill taught in the first class, is one way to activate the PNS.

Table 4.1 provides a simplified list of the effects caused by the PNS and SNS.

The positive effects of relaxation on our bodies have long been studied. In recent decades, there have been many studies that specifically explore the health effects of mindfulness meditation. In addition to its impact on our nervous system, there is research showing that mindfulness training decreases the level of stress hormones (Witek-Janusek et al., 2008) and improves immune function (Davidson et al., 2003). There are studies that show the benefits of mindfulness for persons with cardiac disease, pulmonary disease, chronic pain, fibromyalgia, diabetes, and substance abuse, among many other conditions.

Jon Kabat-Zinn, one of the pioneers of using mindfulness skills to improve medical conditions, examined whether a mindfulness-based stress reduction intervention in psoriasis patients would affect the rate at which their psoriasis cleared (Kabat-Zinn et al., 1998). Thirty-eight patients participated; they were randomly assigned to psoriasis treatment with meditation training or to treatment without the training. They were followed for 13 weeks, during which they received three treatments per week. Patients in the meditation group were guided through meditation using audiotapes. They listened to the first tape before entering the light booth for their treatment and to the second tape during treatment. Their psoriasis lesions were evaluated at four points during the 13 weeks of treatment. This study showed that subjects who underwent the intervention reached the final clearing point significantly more rapidly. This is a pivotal mindfulness study demonstrating how mindfulness training can directly impact our physical health.

TABLE 4.1 The Effects of Activating the Sympathetic and Parasympathetic Branches of the Autonomic Nervous System

Sympathetic Branch	Parasympathetic Branch
Our heart rate increases	Our heart rate decreases
We breathe faster	We breathe more slowly and deeply
Our blood pressure increases	Our blood pressure decreases
Our digestive tract slows down	Our digestion is enhanced
Our far vision improves	Our near vision improves

What about Mindfulness and Mood?

Over the last decade, researchers have begun to explore the relationship between mindfulness and mood/mental health. If mindfulness is helpful for various physical ailments, might it not also have demonstrable benefits for the mind as well? This interest in mindfulness and psychological health has shown up in a variety of ways. In 2007, a symposium was held at Emory University entitled "Mindfulness, Compassion, and the Treatment of Depression," in which leading researchers in mood disorders and meditation as well as the Dalai Lama of Tibet participated. In the January 2008 issue of the journal *Psychiatry*, there was a featured article by Michael McGee (2008) that explored the possible therapeutic benefits of meditation and how it might be used in psychiatric care. In January 2009, Jeff Greeson, a health psychologist with Duke's integrative medicine program, published an article (Greeson, 2009) reviewing the mindfulness literature and listing several mindfulness-based treatment programs that have shown efficacy in treating a range of psychological conditions, including:

- Mindfulness-Based Stress Reduction (MBSR)
- Mindfulness-Based Cognitive Therapy (MBCT)
- Acceptance and Commitment Therapy (ACT)
- Dialectical Behavior Therapy (DBT)
- Mindfulness-Based Eating Awareness Training (MB-EAT)

According to Greeson, these programs help to treat anxiety disorders (MBSR, ACT), recurrent major depression (MBCT), chronic pain (MBSR, ACT), borderline personality disorder (DBT), and binge eating disorder (MB-EAT).

A study evaluating mindfulness-based cognitive therapy and depression was published in 2008 (Kuyken et al., 2008). In this study two groups of people were compared, all of whom had suffered from recurrent depression but had recovered. The subjects were receiving antidepressant medication and were considered to be at risk for relapse. One group simply continued to take their antidepressant. The other group received MBCT in addition to their antidepressant. MBCT combines mindfulness training with cognitive therapy. Cognitive therapy is based on the theory that feelings are influenced by thoughts, and that if we can become more aware of and challenge our negative thoughts, we will be able to feel better emotionally. These study participants were followed for 15 months. Interestingly, patients in the MBCT group who had experienced the largest number of relapses previously (more than three) demonstrated the most benefit, with their rate of recurrence dropping to almost half that of patients who received antidepressant treatment alone. This is a particularly important finding, as recurrent depression can be a very difficult condition to manage. As Greeson notes in his (2009) article, mindfulness training is becoming a foundation of different types of psychotherapy, and studies such as that of Kuyken et al. are demonstrating its positive effects on mental health.

Impact of Emotional States Early in Life on Later Health

Researchers have long been interested in determining if there are behaviors early in life that impact wellness and the quality of life later on. Intuitively, you might suspect that the health habits of young people may affect their long-term health; not surprisingly, there are a number of studies exploring this very topic. There are, for example, two interesting studies that look at the way emotional states in early adulthood impact cardiac health later in life.

In the first study (Siegler, Petersen, Barefoot, & Williams, 1992), the researchers examined the effects of high levels of hostility during adolescence on later cardiac health. Specifically, they assessed 4,710 people who had completed questionnaires when they were in college during the years 1964–1966 to measure how often and how strongly they felt hostile. These same people had their risk factors for heart disease assessed 21–23 years later. The risk factors included cholesterol level, smoking, body mass index (BMI), and caffeine intake. The researchers found that the people with higher hostility scores in college were significantly more likely to have higher than normal cholesterol levels, to smoke, to have a larger than normal BMI, and to consume more caffeine. After taking other factors into consideration, the authors determined there was an association between high hostility in early adulthood and an increased risk for cardiac disease later in life.

The second study (Jantzky, Ahnve, Lundberg, & Hemmingsson, 2010) followed 49,321 Swedish men ages 18–20 who in 1969–1970 underwent a medical examination for military service. Data were collected for depression and anxiety as well as for many lifestyle factors. These men were then followed for 37 years for coronary heart disease (CHD) and heart attack. Anxiety was found to predict CHD independently of other well-known risk factors. This means that even when such risk factors as smoking, diabetes, and a family history of CHD were factored in, anxiety alone predicted CHD. These results suggest that young people who struggle with feelings of anger and hostility, or anxiety and worry, are likely to have more disease later in life than their calmer, happier counterparts. These studies alone do not prove that you can reduce your risk of CHD by learning to maintain a more peaceful state of mind, but they suggest that this may in fact be the case. A more peaceful state of mind has its own immediate rewards, but perhaps it also leads to a longer, healthier life; this is a goal that most emerging adults will agree is worth pursuing.

So, Meditation Is Good for Emerging Adults, But What Do They Themselves Want?

As you saw in chapter 2, emerging adults are living in a time of physical and psychological transitions. They have few commitments and lots of freedom, which means limitless choices. They are trying to make decisions that they recognize will have long-term implications for their lives. These transitions and choices can create their own stresses, which often manifest as worry, difficulty concentrating, insomnia, and general unhappiness; you will most likely hear these concerns from your students when they talk about why they've chosen to learn mindfulness and meditation. Here is what our students say they particularly want from the course:

1. I want to be able to relax and stop worrying all the time.
2. I want to fully enjoy my life.
3. I want to improve my academic performance.
4. I want to sleep better.

We find that many students stay more engaged in the class when they understand that there is scientific evidence that the practice of mindfulness and stress management will help them move toward their important goals. Let's look at these four goals and see what research tells us about how mindfulness and stress management training can help our students achieve them.

1. More Relaxation and Less Worry

Benjamin tells the class that he worries all the time. He feels so anxious that sometimes he thinks he's going crazy. He wants to be able to control his worries better and not let them control him, but he has no idea of how to achieve this. He says he can't imagine not worrying and stressing all the time about his upcoming doctoral defense. "I just want to be less anxious!" He is hoping to gain some quick relief from what he learns in our course.

When it comes to important goals, managing anxiety and stress is perhaps the highest priority for your students. These students have a lot to worry about—everything from exams to relationships to the future. Anxieties about these things can consume a student who is in a highly competitive environment and feels pressured to achieve. Often students are interested in hearing about research related to managing their feeling of stress and calming their bodies and minds. Because this goal is so critical for your students, we will review several studies here, all but one specifically targeting emerging adults.

On occasion we have medical students in our classes, and their stress level tends to be very high. One study explores the effect of an MBSR program on distress in medical students (Rosenzweig, Reibel, Greeson, Brainard, & Hojat, 2003). A total of 140 second-year medical students completed this program, and 162, the control group, participated in a seminar on complementary medicine. At the end of the two programs, the MBSR students reported significant improvement in overall mood and significant decrease in distress compared to the control group. Another group of researchers (Shapiro, Schwartz, & Bonner, 1998) studied premedical and medical students. Seventy-eight students were divided into control and intervention groups. The intervention was an 8-week meditation-based stress reduction program. The students completed study questionnaires before the intervention and afterward; the study was designed so that the final questionnaires were given out during an exam period, when all of the students were stressed. The results of this study are impressive: the students who participated in the intervention had significantly lower anxiety, depression, and distress and significantly higher empathy and spirituality.

Deckro et al. (2002) examined the effect of a 6-week mind–body intervention on college students' psychological distress, anxiety, and perception of stress. Sixty-three students participated in the program, called "Maximize Your Potential," and were compared to 65 students in the control group. The intervention consisted of six 90-minute group-training sessions in relaxation response and cognitive-behavioral skills. The relaxation skills included diaphragmatic breathing, guided imagery, progressive muscle relation, brief relation exercises, yoga, and mindfulness. The cognitive-behavioral skills included identifying automatic thoughts, challenging cognitive distortion, affirmation, and goal setting. The authors found that the trained students demonstrated significantly greater decreases in psychological distress, stated anxiety (how students feel at the present moment), and perceived stress.

There is a fascinating study (Oman, Shapiro, Thoresen, Plante, & Flinders, 2008) evaluating the effects of a meditation program on stress, rumination, forgiveness, and hope in college students. The study included 29 participants in the study group and 15 in the control group. Eight weeks after the training and again 8 weeks later, the students completed scales measuring stress, rumination, hopefulness, and the ability to forgive others who had hurt or disappointed them. The students who underwent one of the two 8-week, 90-minute/week training programs participated in either MBSR or Easwaran's Eight-Point Program. (The latter is a program developed by a well-known meditation teacher, Eknath Easwaran, that is similar to MBSR). Students in both programs showed significant benefits on stress and forgiveness.

Manzoni, Pagnini, Castelnuovo, and Molinari (2008) looked at the cumulative data on the effects on anxiety of helping people calm themselves. They performed a large analysis (meta-analysis) of 27 studies published between 1997 and 2007 that had assessed the effects of relaxation training on anxiety. They synthesized the data from these studies and found that when compared to control groups who did not receive some type of relaxation training (progressive relaxation, autogenic training, and meditation), those who received the relaxation intervention showed significant improvement. The highest demonstrated efficacy was for meditation. This meta-analysis supports our experience that learning to meditate and developing mindfulness-based relaxation skills are effective approaches to reducing stress, anxiety, and worry.

As we noted above, our students need quick relief from their anxiety. Therefore, we teach anxiety-relieving stress management skills that can be used in the moment. In Part Two of this book, we will teach you these skills. Meanwhile, if you are curious, they are described in our course syllabus in Appendix B. One of these skills is breathing from the belly, also called *diaphragmatic breathing*, which has a number of physiological effects that help reduce anxiety and stress and improve mood. These effects include the following:

- We increase the amount of oxygen entering our lungs and thus our bodies.
- Our heart rate slows.

- Our blood pressure drops.
- We stimulate the vagus nerve, which runs through the diaphragm; this is our calming nerve that activates the PNS.

There are many research studies exploring the physiological effects of diaphragmatic breathing, for example, in people with lung disease or heart disease. The popular press has also picked up on this interest in using the breath to calm the body. In December 2010, National Public Radio produced a program called "Just Breathe: Body Has a Built-In Stress Reliever" (http://www.npr.org/2010/12/06/131734718/just-breathe-body-has-a-built-in-stress-reliever). In this program, Gretchen Cuda interviews three experts about breath work and its effects on health. The interviewer performs both deep, slow breathing and the faster *firebreathing* (called *dynamic breathing* in our course) and learns from the experts how these kinds of breathing positively affect health.

Another mind–body or stress-management skill that we teach is *guided imagery*. Guided imagery is used successfully in the traditional medical world to reduce pain, assist in healing, and reduce morbidity. Brain scanning can show us what happens in the brain when we imagine or visualize a beautiful, comforting place. When we engage all of our senses to imagine vivid images, as we teach in our model, the part of the brain for vision "lights up" on the scan. When we imagine hearing a sound, the hearing part of the brain lights up. We can "trick" the brain into thinking that we really are in a beautiful, peaceful, or comforting place, and the body responds as if we actually are there. A graduate student in our class who was particularly drawn to this skill discovered that if she felt stressed while working in the lab, she could take out a few minutes to imagine herself relaxing in her favorite vacation spot. After just a few minutes of working with this image, she found that she was much more relaxed and ready to proceed with her work.

There is good evidence that guided imagery can have benefits for our health and well-being. One such study (Tusek, Church, Strong, & Fazio, 1997), which we often cite in our class on guided imagery, measures the impact that guided imagery has on recovery from colon surgery. The study compared patients who were given training in guided imagery before surgery with those who were not. The intervention subjects spent time listening to a guided imagery tape 3 days preoperatively and during each of the first 6 postoperative days. These subjects showed a number of benefits from practicing guided imagery: they had less anxiety and pain postoperatively, less need for narcotics to control pain, an earlier first bowel movement (an important indicator that the colon was recovering), and earlier discharge from the hospital. This study nicely demonstrates the mind–body connection and reinforces that training the mind can have benefits for physical health.

Jain and colleagues (2007) compared mindfulness meditation with relaxation training in college students. Eighty-three students who reported distress were divided into a control group, a relaxation group, and a mindfulness group. The researchers measured psychological distress, positive states of mind, distractive and ruminative thoughts and behaviors, and spiritual experience. The study found that the two interventions reduced distress and improved positive mood states. The authors note that mindfulness training seemed to have a particular effect on reducing ruminating and distracting behaviors. Students often report feeling plagued by ruminative thoughts, so we devote a significant amount of class time to helping them begin to eliminate this problem. In fact, the guided meditations in both the third and fourth classes are devoted to helping students free themselves from their ruminations and the uncomfortable feelings they produce. Generally, the students report that this is an area in which they feel they have made good progress by the time the course is over.

2. Greater Sense of Well-being

"I just want to be happier" says Wei, a freshman, in the first class. She says that her days go by with so many things to handle that she feels stressed all the time. She reports feeling much happier in high school, when she had time to do all the things she loves. But now at Duke she feels that she has to study much harder, and she is afraid of falling behind. She also worries about the major she will choose, and about her career path, and is thinking a lot about which choices will make her happy.

As we discussed in chapter 2, the quest for happiness is a goal near and dear to the hearts of most emerging adults. A study published in *Science* (Killingsworth & Gilbert, 2010) took a very interesting approach to finding out what actually makes us happy as we go about our daily lives. The researchers created an iPhone application called *trackyourhappiness,* which would interrupt the study participants randomly and ask them certain questions. This kind of research is called *experience sampling;* the participants' phones would chime at random intervals during the day and they would be asked: "How are you feeling right now, on a 1–100 scale?" "What are you doing right now?" "Are you thinking about something other than what you are currently doing?" In answering this last question, the participants could respond "no"; "yes, something pleasant"; "yes, something neutral"; or "yes, something unpleasant." The researchers tracked about 5,000 people and used 2,250 in the study.

The basic result of this study is no surprise to those who practice mindfulness meditation: we are happiest when our thoughts are on the task at hand. Another way to say this is that we are happiest when we are being mindful, that is, present. And the study shows that it basically doesn't matter what we're doing; if we're being mindful, we are happier. So, doing a chore such as washing the dishes and thinking about a beach trip does not make us happier than actually being present with the dishwashing. And in this study, what is the activity during which our minds wander least? No surprise to our emerging adults: having sex, or "making love," as the researchers refer to it. This finding alone will get your 20-somethings to sit up and pay attention. Hopefully, they will also get the main message of the study: paying attention to your present moment experience, no matter what it is, increases your happiness.

Another study, a classic in the field of mindfulness (Davidson et al., 2003), is one that we often speak about in class. It demonstrates the positive effect of meditation on our emotional state and on our immune system. The subjects of the study were healthy company employees who had agreed to participate. The researchers provided an 8-week training program in mindfulness; the control group was made up of employees who did not participate in the training. There were 25 individuals in each group. The effects of meditation on brain function were studied by using brain scans to determine whether significant changes occur in the brain as a result of meditation practice. The researchers were interested in the left-sided anterior portion of the brain, which when activated has been shown to be associated with the experience of positive emotions such as contentment and pleasure. They measured brain activity before, immediately after, and 4 months after the training program. After the program, the researchers vaccinated both groups with influenza vaccine, measuring the strength of their immune response to the vaccination.

There were two interesting findings in this study. First, the meditators showed a significant increase in activation in the left-sided anterior portion of the brain. Second, the meditators produced more antibodies to the flu vaccine, which suggests that meditating helped their immune systems respond more effectively to the vaccine.

A third study (Feldman, Greeson & Senville, 2010) approaches the subject of happiness from another perspective: can mindfulness training help us change our relationship to our thoughts through acceptance and objectivity, and thus reduce the negativity in our lives and perhaps help us be happier? This study involved 190 undergraduates at an all-women's college, who were divided into three groups for three different interventions: mindful breathing, loving-kindness meditation, and progressive muscle relaxation. The researchers wanted to see if the mindfulness training helped the students to *decenter* (i.e., to view their thoughts with some objectivity) more than the other two interventions. Viewing our thoughts more objectively is one way of getting less caught up in our worries and fears. After each intervention, the students completed measures of decentering, reporting how often they had repetitive thoughts and how often they reacted negatively to these thoughts. The students in the mindful breathing group reported increased decentering compared to those in the other two groups.

All of these studies demonstrate in different ways that mindfulness and meditation have the potential to increase feelings of happiness and contentment, an outcome that is important to emerging adults.

3. Improved Academic Performance

Robin is a junior who has just gotten her first C in a course in her major. She has never before in her life gotten a grade lower than B, and she is used to achieving mostly A's. She has a vague feeling that she's in a vicious cycle because she is so stressed about her grades that she's not sleeping well and can't concentrate or focus on her work as she used to do. A counselor at the student counseling center has recommended the meditation program for her. At check-in, she tells us that she needs to feel less stressed and be able to work hard at the same time; she doesn't know how to do this.

Academic performance is always on the minds of students. You know, if you work in any kind of academic setting, that much of what the students value is measured in grades, and they believe that they need excellent grades in order to achieve whatever goal is next for them. The pressure can be intense.

There is growing evidence that mindfulness and meditation can help students improve their academic performance. Franco, Manas, Cangas, and Gallego (2010) studied the effects of mindfulness training on academic performance and anxiety in high school students ages 16–18. Sixty-one students participated in the study, divided into a control group and an intervention group. They filled in questionnaires about anxiety, and their tutors supplied their first-quarter grades. The students in the intervention group then underwent 10 weeks of training in meditation, 1½ hours per week. At the end of 3 months, all of the students again completed the questionnaires and their grades were assessed. The trained students showed significant academic improvement in all subjects, as well as significantly less anxiety. These results, showing that students can both perform better and be less anxious, are very important and support one of the fundamental teachings of our program: students can feel less stress and be more productive, even in the context of their very busy lives.

Scientific studies have begun to try to determine what is actually going on in the brain as benefits from mindfulness training and meditation begin to emerge. One way of doing this is to use brain scans to look at the brains of meditators and see if it is possible to identify changes in brain structure or function that may be the result of meditation. Holzel and her group (2011) examined brain changes produced by meditation and found that meditation produces measurable changes in brain structure, even after a relatively short amount of practice,. The researchers studied a group of subjects who had practiced mindfulness meditation for 30 minutes a day for just 8 weeks. They measured the density of gray matter in the subjects' brains both before and after the 8 weeks of meditation. Gray matter in the brain is comprised primarily of the cell bodies of neurons and other support cells. Thinning of the gray matter is generally associated with a decline in brain function, as in patients with dementia or even, to some degree, in normal aging; thickening of the gray matter is generally associated with improvement in brain function. The researchers found that in the meditators, gray matter thickened in the region of the brain most critical for memory, the hippocampus. Interestingly, they also found thinning of the gray matter in the brain region associated with the production of feelings of anxiety and stress: the amygdala. These findings suggest that even a brief period of meditation can begin to adjust the brain's balance away from anxiety and stress and toward improved memory and concentration, perhaps producing improvement in academic performance.

4. Sleeping Better and Feeling More Rested

Lynne has come to our class mainly because she is having great difficulty getting to sleep at night. She goes to bed feeling tired but then can't stop thinking about all the things she has to do. She then feels anxious because she's afraid she won't be at her best when facing all the demands of the next day. She feels so much pressure that she lies awake for hours before finally falling asleep. David, on the other hand, has no problem falling asleep, but he can't stay asleep; he often wakes up at night worrying about the next day's challenges and tasks.

Lynne's and David's experiences are common ones for the students who come to our classes. You will often hear students mention in the first class that their difficulty sleeping is one of their biggest problems and their reason for coming to Koru. One study (Gaultney, 2010) found that 27% of college students are at risk for a sleep disorder. Either because they can't sleep or because they feel too busy to take the time to sleep, chronic sleep deprivation is common in emerging adults. We see this phenomenon in our classes, where students complain of exhaustion and at times fall asleep during the guided meditation sessions.

In one study, Yook et al. (2008) examined how Mindfulness-Based Cognitive Therapy (MBCT) might be helpful in treating patients with anxiety and insomnia. Nineteen participants completed 8 weeks of MBCT. Their postintervention scale scores showed a significant improvement in sleep quality, as well as a reduction in anxiety, rumination, and depression.

Ong and Sholtes (2010) explored the benefits of a mindfulness-based therapy for insomnia (MBT-I). Their program includes eight sessions and one all-day retreat and involves formal mindfulness meditation, discussion of how to apply the meditation to insomnia, a lecture about sleep/wake physiology, and instructions for sleep hygiene. The participants are encouraged to meditate regularly between the weekly sessions, using Jon Kabat-Zinn's "Full Catastrophe Living" as their text. This article describes a case illustration of one participant in the program and reports that after the program she doubled her sleep time and reported higher sleep quality and fewer negative beliefs about sleep. She also reported less daytime sleepiness and fatigue. Her approach to her insomnia changed to one of increased acceptance and less distress.

This patient's experience is similar to what we see in our classes. Often students report that their sleep improves as they develop the ability to calm their bodies and quiet their minds.

Attention Deficit Disorder and Eating Disorders

Before we close this chapter, let's look at two disorders that are prevalent during emerging adulthood: attention deficit disorder (ADD) and eating disorders. It is not uncommon for students struggling with these disorders to enroll in Koru.

Students often cite a desire to improve their concentration and focus as a reason for learning mindfulness; this need is particularly great in students struggling with ADD. Mindfulness training addresses focus and attention in a fundamental way, training students to become aware of and focus their thoughts. In one study (Tang et al., 2007), the researchers wanted to find out if a short period of training in meditation could improve attention. They trained 40 undergraduates for 20 minutes over 5 days in an integrative body–mind training that included body relaxation, breath adjustment, mental imagery, and mindfulness. The findings showed that, compared to the controls, the trained students showed significantly greater improvement in attention as well as in control of stress (as measured by the level of the stress hormone cortisol). In addition to the positive effect on attention, the researchers noted that the trained students had lower anxiety, depression, anger, stress, fatigue, and conflict, as well as what the authors called "higher vigor." This study is important because it demonstrates that even a short period of training can result in improved attention.

A number of researchers have specifically studied the use of mindfulness as a treatment for identified ADD. Hesslinger and colleagues (2002) developed a mindfulness-based cognitive therapy program to treat ADD. In their pilot study, the treatment produced a reduction in the symptoms of ADD in their participants. Zylowska and colleagues (2007) also explored the feasibility of using mindfulness meditation to treat ADD. After a period of training with mindfulness, their patients showed improved scores on tests of attention and reported a reduction in their symptoms of ADD.

A number of other mindfulness-based treatments are being studied or are now available for ADD. Given that the main task of mindfulness meditation involves training the mind to steady and focus, it is not surprising that this is a useful practice for individuals who find it difficult to sustain their attention on challenging tasks. One of the symptoms of severe stress is decreased ability to concentrate and focus, so your students don't have to have ADD in order to experience this benefit of mindfulness meditation.

Eating disorders represent another serious health concern among emerging adults, and there is growing evidence that mindfulness-based treatments can be effective for a range of eating disorders. One study (Proulx, 2008) was performed with six college-age women with bulimia who participated in an 8-week mindfulness-based eating disorder treatment group. The author reported that the women experienced transformative change, developing greater compassion and acceptance as well as self-awareness; they also reported feeling less stressed and said that they could handle stress better.

A pilot study (Dalen, Smith, Shelley, Sloan, Leahigh, & Begay, 2010) examined how a mindfulness-based program affects weight, eating behavior, and psychological outcomes in people with obesity. Eight young men participated in the study, completing a 6-week program in mindfulness meditation, mindful eating, and group discussion. The researchers collected data before the intervention, at completion, and 3 months later. This study had several statistically significant results when the data at baseline were compared to later data: increased mindfulness and cognitive restraint concerning eating, as well as decreases in weight, eating disinhibition, binge eating, depression, perceived stress, physical symptoms, negative affect, and levels of C-reactive protein (a measure of stress).

These studies are consistent with our experience that students who feel out of control when eating (binge eating and bulimia), as well as students who overcontrol their eating (anorexia), can benefit from becoming more mindful of their emotional and physical responses to hunger and eating.

The mindfulness skill we teach in our fourth class is an eating meditation. *Eating meditation* is a mindfulness practice and a skill that has multiple benefits. Eating more slowly and paying more attention to our eating allows our brains to register when we are full and to signal us to stop eating. When we eat too fast, the brain cannot catch up and the signal of fullness comes after we have consumed too much. It takes our stomach about 20 minutes of eating to release the hormones signaling to the brain that we are full. Eating more slowly can also improve our digestion. Digestion starts in the mouth, so if we chew more slowly, we give the stomach a head start.

Eating mindfully allows us to enjoy our food more. When we eat, we engage the pleasure center in our brains. When your students start to pay attention to the thoughts and feelings that arise when they eat, they will likely report that they have a multitude of judgments about their eating and their bodies; mindfulness training can teach them to release their judgments, focusing their attention instead on the pleasant physical sensations evoked by eating delicious food. Thus, teaching emerging adults to eat mindfully can create a range of benefits, both physical and psychological. For emerging adults with eating disorders, these changes can be particularly meaningful.

Final Thoughts

As we end our review of the scientific literature, one last point is worth making. It is true that it can be helpful to use this information to broaden the students' learning and to motivate them to persist. It is important for them to understand that there is solid scientific evidence demonstrating improvements in physical and psychological health for individuals who develop skills in meditation and mindfulness. At the same time, you will find that it is important to remind the students that their personal experience is their best and most meaningful "research." The only way for them to really understand the benefits of mindfulness and meditation is to try it for themselves. Encourage the students to reserve judgment and pay close attention as they persist with their daily meditation homework over the 4 weeks of the course. Ask them to consider the following: As you gain experience with mindfulness and meditation, do you feel more or less stressed? More or less peaceful? More or less engaged with your day-to-day experience? The best measure of the worth of this work is the transformation that occurs in our lives as we experience the power of living mindfully.

Finally, let's consider the importance of something as simple as smiling. Yes, we do teach the students to smile during their gatha training (see chapter 7). And, yes, there is research on smiling. There is an excellent review article in the *New York Times*, written by Daniel Goleman in 1989, called "A Feel-Good Theory: A Smile Affects Mood." Goleman reviews the history of those thinkers, including Charles Darwin and William James, who have pondered the question of how the movement of our facial muscles affects our mood and emotions. Is a smile a result of our feeling good or can a smile help us feel happy? Or both? This article explores theories about these questions. It cites two researchers who have done a lot of work in this field, Paul Ekman and Robert Zajonc, and you will find articles by them in the References section at the end of this book. However, in the spirit of ending this chapter with a smile, we won't burden you with research studies. Instead, we recommend that you go to this link to read the entertaining Goleman article: http://query.nytimes.com/gst/fullpage.html?res=950DE4D71F3AF93BA25754C0A96F948260 &pagewanted=all.

And with a smile, let's move on to the chapters that describe Koru, the model we have developed at Duke University.

PART TWO

Koru

The Course Specifics

Structure and Logistics

When we consider the format, structure, and logistics of the Koru course, we are struck by how even these practical aspects of our model make it possible for students to learn the practice and skills we are teaching. A critical aspect of the model is the emphasis on both meditation and mindfulness-based stress-management skills. Although learning the skill of mindfulness meditation is a necessary component of the transformation we are guiding students toward, by itself it has not proved sufficient for the majority of emerging adults we have taught. The skills-based practice you will give them provides them with tools that they can use to manage their stress levels when the acute need arises; the meditation practice leads them toward fundamental changes in the way they approach their day-to-day experience.

Anne provides an excellent example of a student who needs help with her stress:

Anne is a 24-year-old graduate student in a doctoral program in biomedical engineering. She spends long hours in her lab as well as in class. She is also a teaching assistant. She has come to Duke from Vanderbilt, another prestigious and competitive university, and she has been used to the pace and stress of her life. However, she is beginning to feel that she can no longer manage the demands of her doctoral program without significant stress and anxiety. A few years ago, she came in contact with meditation through a friend, but she found it impossible to sit still on her own and meditate. She has also tried yoga and found it helpful, but she cannot fit a yoga class into her busy life. She feels trapped in her stressful and demanding life but is willing to try to make a change. She heard about Koru, and she went to Duke's counseling center's Web site and signed up. She likes the fact that the course is only four sessions long and thinks that she can commit to this schedule. But she feels pessimistic about her ability to inject some kind of meditative practice into her life.

We will come back to Anne later in this chapter to illustrate how a typical student might experience the structural aspects of the Koru model.

CHAPTER 5: KEY POINTS

- Recruitment for the class involves advertising the class widely to capture as diverse a group of participants as possible.
- Teachers communicate with their students frequently before the course begins and between classes, so you will need to get phone numbers and e-mails when students register.
- From the very beginning, emphasize to the students that attendance and practice are mandatory. Participants must be able to commit to attendance at all four classes.
- Before the course starts, confirm registration with each participant. Keep a wait list to draw on if any initial registrants withdraw.
- There are a number of tools you will use for teaching, including a syllabus, meditation logs, written evaluations, and resource guides. You'll find examples of these in the appendices of this book.

Koru is designed specifically for students like Anne, who live under severe time pressures and who are used to classroom demands such as homework. The format and structure are inspired by the model for teaching mind–body skills developed at the Center for Mind-Body Medicine (CMBM), but we have modified it for our student population. (Please see Appendix A for a description of the CMBM program.) We have also incorporated a number of elements of Jon Kabat-Zinn's Mindfulness-Based Stress Reduction Program. The course is composed of four classes lasting for 75 minutes each. Twelve students are enrolled in each course. In this chapter, we will consider the logistics and tools that are part of the practical implementation of Koru, and we will "check in" with Anne.

Time Frame and Class Size

Over the years, we have experimented with the size and time structure of our course. Regarding class size, we have learned that **12 is the optimal number of participants.** Larger classes keep the students from bonding well, and smaller classes don't produce a powerful enough group dynamic. Twelve seems perfect, so we suggest you aim for about this number. Sometimes a particularly persuasive student will convince us to let him or her join an already full class, but in general, we have found that when the group grows to 14 or more, it starts to lose some of its impact.

Regarding the time structure, our experience is that **four classes of 75 minutes is the most effective schedule.** Three classes don't provide sufficient training and experience; five classes have led to higher attrition rates. Shorter classes don't allow enough teaching time during check-in. Interestingly, the most frequently cited recommendation for improvement by the students on their evaluations is an enthusiastic "more classes!" However, when we have tried adding classes, we have found that the students did not attend all the classes consistently. We have decided that four classes works best; the students finish the course wanting more, the best possible attitude with which to leave them.

Finding a time that works for the students is always a challenge. If you are in a college setting, you will quickly realize that morning classes are doomed to failure because the undergraduates just can't get out of bed. **Classes at noon or at the end of the workday are often convenient for students.** When planning your course, carefully consider the schedules of the participants you are hoping to recruit, and try to choose a time that will likely work for the most people.

Recruitment

Once your Koru course is up and running, students like Anne will learn about it through the grapevine. Until that happens, recruitment will be a more active process. If you work in a university or college setting, there are readily available options for recruitment. As we discussed in chapter 3, the goal of recruitment is to **ensure that a diverse group of students learns about your class** and have the opportunity to enroll. Contacting the various **organizations and agencies that serve student groups** is a great place to start. Most college and university campuses have organizations that reach out to and support students who differ in some way from the dominant culture on the campus. For example, it is common to find organizations for African-American students, Latino/Latina students, international students, lesbian/gay/bisexual/transgender students, and students with different religious affiliations, to name just a few. In general, these organizations are always looking for ways to help the students they represent manage their stress better, and they will probably be happy to advertise your class. **The student health center and the counseling center** are also great places to advertise; you may get referrals for students suffering from a wide range of stress-related conditions from these agencies.

Advertising on **Web sites and through e-mail lists** is the easiest way to target a large number of potential participants, so that is always a good place to start, but don't forget the less technical forms of advertising. **Flyers** placed in strategic locales on campus, such as the library and dormitories, can capture the attention of students. Also, students tend to read the **student newspaper,** where a well-placed ad can draw additional participants. Every campus is different, so be creative and take advantage of whatever resources are at your disposal. Personal referrals tend to have a big impact, so make sure you **talk to a wide range of staff,** administrators, and even resident advisers, to get them excited about your course. You might even consider inviting staff to participate in a demonstration class, where you introduce them to mindfulness and teach them one or two skills from Koru. A staff member who has experienced the class will be a more enthusiastic source of referrals for you.

If you don't work on a college or university campus, but instead work with some other agency that serves emerging adults, consider the suggestions above and see if they can be adapted to suit your particular agency. Take advantage of whatever outreach methods your agency uses to communicate with its clients. Web sites, newsletters, and e-mail lists are obvious places to start, but look for other ways to get the word out, such as announcements at weekly meetings. Again, remember that personal connections are a great source of referrals, so make the effort to meet with as many people as possible who might be a source of referrals.

In the fall of 2010, we started asking registrants on the Duke University Web site to tell us how they heard about the program. As of this writing, we have obtained this information for two classes. For the first one, half of the students heard about it from their counselors at Duke's counseling center; the rest of the sources were spread out in seven other places (such as e-mail flyers and word of mouth). For the second class, only two recommendations came from counselors and the rest from three other places. We will continue to collect these data and would advise you to establish a way to monitor these important sources of information yourself as you consider how best to advertise the course.

Registration

Once you have decided how to advertise your class, it is important to consider how to register the students for the class. It is imperative that students **register in advance.** You will need to communicate with them before the course begins to **confirm their participation** and provide them with some precourse information. You will also want to keep track of the number of students who register and **start a wait list** once you have confirmed a maximum of 12 participants for the course. Registration can be done electronically or through a sign-up sheet. Be sure to get contact information from your participants, including both e-mail and phone numbers.

If you work on a college or university campus, arrange for your agency's **Web site** to prominently display a link for information and registration for the class. On your Web site, it is important to state that participation in all four classes is mandatory. List the class schedule and either a link or an e-mail address for registering. Adding a little information about mindfulness can also be helpful. For example, on our Web site, we mention that Koru is for students who are feeling stressed and pressured or who just want to get more satisfaction from their college experience. We also provide an e-mail address so that they can contact us for more information if they have questions.

As noted above, we recommend a maximum class size of 12 students but advise you to keep a **wait list** of interested students once your class is full. Let the students on the wait list know that you will contact them if you have an opening. In our experience, it is fairly common for one or more students to find that something emerges in their busy lives to prevent them from committing to all four classes. We ask these students to consider signing up for a later course and invite the next student on the wait list to join the class.

We often hear from students, usually in the form of e-mails, who have questions or concerns before they complete their registration. Some of these e-mails are touching in the way they express the student's eagerness. Here is an e-mail we received from a student requesting to be in the class:

> My name is NN and I am a senior this year. I have been interested in Mindfulness Meditation for quite some time now and wanted to take this 4-week course you are offering but up until a day ago I had a class scheduled at the same time. I have now dropped the class and really want to enroll in this 4-week course.
>
> I just finished meeting with [a counselor], and she said that the course was already full. I am so disappointed because I have had my eye on this for some time and feel that it would be really beneficial to my mental health. I think I would just benefit from sitting in the back of the room – I won't say anything, and no one will know that I am there – but if there is any, any way at all I could just sit in, I would be so grateful to you.
>
> If there is any possibility of you making "magic" happen for me, I would be indebted to you. This is the one thing I really want to learn before I leave college, and I don't know when I will get another chance. Also, this has been a rough year for me, and I truly believe that a course like this could help me turn everything around. Please consider just allowing me to sit in, even if it's not to participate.

If you've been able to advertise the class widely, you can expect a nice mix of students with a broad range of reasons for joining. We typically have both undergraduate and graduate students, as well as students from Duke's professional schools. Here is a typical roster of students and what they said as they introduced themselves in the first class (fictional names):

1. Sam says he is attending for help with anxiety and depression; he is in the Divinity School, hoping to become a pastor, and a counselor from the student counseling center had recommended Jon Kabat-Zinn's book *Wherever You Go, There You Are* (1994).
2. Roderigo, originally from Peru, is a Ph.D. student who says he needs help with concentration and who has read *The Power of Now* by Eckhart Tolle (1999).
3. Takame is a freshman and feels overwhelmed by her classes. She is afraid she won't be able to manage her studies.
4. Ming, from China, is a senior who says she needs help with stress and wants to be able to focus in the moment.
5. Jocelyn is a 6th-year Ph.D. student in biology and is worried about the future. She doesn't know if she will be able to get a job, and she says she can't stop thinking about this.

6. Sonia is a sophomore, originally from India, who says she worries all the time and can't sleep. She says she wants to be happier.

7. Lisa is a graduate student in literature and wants to be able to concentrate her mind and tap into the unconscious.

8. Tomas, from the Czech Republic, is a 3rd-year physical therapy student who says that his anxiety is out of control.

9. Elisabeth is a 2nd-year medical student who is facing clinical work and being on call and wants to learn how to manage this kind of stress.

10. Aadesh is a 5th-year graduate student who wants to be able to control his thoughts.

11. Omar is a senior who is planning to attend graduate school and wants to learn how to manage stress better.

12. Carinna is a sophomore who is interested in learning more about meditation; she has meditated in the past.

Communication with the Students

Let's check in with Anne, who registered for the course but has concerns about how it will help her manage her stress and anxiety:

> Anne has gotten the required book but has not had time to read it and, indeed, has forgotten when the first class meets. She is wondering if she should just forget about it or e-mail the teacher when she receives a confirmation e-mail about the course. She responds that she intends to participate and wonders who else will be in the class. She is feeling alone with all her worries and stress. Just before the first class, another e-mail arrives; it is warm and welcoming and also contains a quotation from the text. Anne feels slightly comforted, likes the quote, and now finds herself looking forward to the course. She has also decided to start reading the book, since the e-mail asked everyone to bring a quote from it.

Almost all of our students are like Anne. They are very busy and have complex schedules. They are members of the tech generation, and electronic communication suits them best. You will need to determine the best form of communication for your students, but you are likely to find that **e-mailing and/or texting** is the most effective method. Make an e-mail group for the class so that you can easily contact the entire group. An important part of the Koru model is regular communication with the students for the purpose of keeping them motivated and engaged with the material between classes; you'll want to make it as easy as possible to send out group communications. See Appendix D for examples of our e-mail communication with our students.

The communication with students should begin as soon as they register, letting them know that you've received their registration and reminding them that they need to commit to all four classes if they want to participate in the course. About 2 weeks before the class starts, send an **e-mail** to the group, asking them to confirm that they are planning to participate in the class. This e-mail also mentions the required text. If you don't receive an e-mail reply from certain students, try to contact them by phone or e-mail before giving their spot to another student on the wait list. Because we place such emphasis on students committing to attending all four classes, we strongly recommend that you put time and energy into getting a clear confirmation from each student before the course begins.

Despite our emphasis on perfect attendance, it is fairly common for students to have to miss a class for some reason, despite their best intentions to attend all four. If a student misses the first class, we recommend contacting the student and determining whether he feels able to make the remaining three classes. If he feels that he can and still wishes to do so, you should invite him to join the group for the remaining classes. If the student no longer wishes to participate, you can consider letting a student on the wait list join the course for the last three classes. Similarly, if a student misses one of the later classes, you can touch base with her during the week and invite her to return to the next class. If, however, a student misses two classes, she has probably missed too much of the required material and would be better served by being encouraged to enroll in a later Koru course.

About 1 week before the first class, you can begin introducing the students to the concepts you will teach them by sending them a **reminder e-mail** that includes a quotation about mindfulness. This e-mail reminds them yet again that attendance at all four classes is required. Other requirements, such as daily mindfulness practice, are also outlined. In this e-mail, you should also remind the students to purchase in advance the book for the course, *Wherever You Go, There You Are* by Jon Kabat- Zinn. Ask the students to start reading the book and to bring a meaningful quote to the first class. This gets the students to start reading about mindfulness in advance of the class. Our students typically comply with this request, and we have found the quotations they bring to be a source of inspiration and information for their fellow students.

Anne finds, when she starts reading, that the book speaks to her. She is beginning to understand that mindfulness practice is not going to require a lot of stress and strain; it is more about acceptance. This appeals to her, and she laughs at herself because she has difficulty picking one quote from the many that she likes for class.

Communication with the students between classes should continue throughout the course. Plan to send at least **one e-mail to the students each week**, reminding them to do their mindfulness homework and sharing more information or inspiring quotes about mindfulness. This serves to keep them engaged and motivated to continue practicing throughout the week.

Setting

The e-mails have emphasized punctuality, so Anne makes sure to arrive a few minutes early. As she enters the room, she finds that several others are already there as well. Anne feels a bit shy but takes her place in the circle of chairs. She has been welcomed by the teachers, and she feels she can let down some of her guard. She finds the room peaceful and welcomes this tranquility in the midst of her demanding life.

Find a location for your classes that is large enough to comfortably hold up to 14 or so **chairs placed in a circle**. The circle is important so that everyone can see everyone else and feel part of the group. If you have two teachers, they should sit in the circle halfway around from each other. A **clock** on the wall that is easily viewed by one of the teachers is helpful for making sure that the class stays on track. There should be no table in the circle so that the space is free for movement. Adjust the **lighting** so that it is not too bright; candles are lovely but are not allowed in all settings. Relaxing **music** playing in the background as the students come in is a nice addition. Our goal is to create a calming atmosphere. You may have other ideas about how to set up the room so that it is welcoming, warm, and serene.

Structure

We believe that maintaining a clear structure is important, so we recommend that you **start and end each class on time.** Only for the first class do we wait a few minutes for latecomers. The students should be told at the first class that punctuality is important and that they should come in quietly if they are late. It's a good idea to post a sign with this information on the door to the room. While the students are gathering, you may want to chat informally with them, perhaps asking them about their experience with meditation, as a way of helping them feel comfortable while waiting for the class to start.

Each of the four classes is organized the same way. During each class, the students are taught a mindfulness-based tool or skill for managing stress. Also, training and practice in mindfulness meditation are provided in each class. In chapters 6 through 9, you will find the details of each skill that is taught, and we have provided scripts for the guided meditations. Though the specifics of the skill taught and the meditation training differ in each class, the following components and their order do not vary:

- After everyone has gathered, welcome the students and then instruct them to get into meditation positions for a **5-minute meditation**. We use chairs for our class, as that seems to be the arrangement that most people find comfortable. If you have meditation cushions or benches available, it is fine to use them if the students prefer.
- **Check-in** is next, during which each student is given the opportunity to talk about his or her experience and ask questions. This is when you will do most of your formal teaching: in the context of students' questions and concerns. For the first class, check-in consists of the students introducing themselves and describing what they hope to gain from the course. In subsequent classes, the students report on their experience with their mindfulness practice over the preceding week. Importantly, you should also participate in check-in, sharing your goals in the first class and your experience with mindfulness and meditation in subsequent classes.

- After check-in, you will **introduce the mindfulness skill for the week and then lead the students in practicing the skill**. There is brief informal teaching about the skill (that we call a *didactic*) and perhaps a mention of scientific studies related to it. Then you practice the skill as a group.

- After the group practices the skill, ask for general **feedback** about it. Sometimes this takes only a couple of minutes, sometimes longer. You will want to play this by ear, making sure to allow time for the guided meditation.

- You will introduce the **guided meditation** with a brief teaching about the aspect of meditation that will be emphasized in the particular class. Aim to allow 15 minutes for this meditation.

- When the meditation is over, you say goodbye, give out logs for the week, and remind the students to continue practicing mindfulness as they leave the room and move to whatever activities await them.

> Like many of our students, Anne finds that she enjoys check-in. She is discovering that she is not alone with her *issues,* that others are struggling with their own anxieties. She is impressed that the other students are so forthcoming about how their meditation practice is going, with its inevitable ups and downs. She also gains ideas from the teachers and students about how to help her keep up her own practice.

Tools

1. *Required text.* Kabat-Zinn's book *Wherever You Go, There You Are* (1994) is the required text for Koru. We have found it to be a fundamental and excellent resource for the class. You can use the syllabus to assign specific readings from the text for each class. As noted above, you can ask the students to bring a favorite quote from the book to the first class. Consider doing this for the last class as well. During check-in, encourage the students to give feedback on the book, and offer some of your own favorite quotes from it during class. You may have another book that you prefer to use, but plan to use it in the way we have described here.

> Anne feels inspired and encouraged by the required text. It's easy to read, and it is nonjudgmental. It has helped Anne feel that she can really learn to meditate, and she is beginning to understand more about having compassion for herself as she learns.

2. *Syllabus.* It is helpful for the students to have an idea of how the class will unfold over subsequent weeks. Therefore, you should plan to provide a syllabus at the first class. The syllabus should include a review of the structure and requirements for the course, the required readings for each class, a description of the mindfulness skill that will be taught in each class, and some teaching about these skills. A copy of our syllabus is provided in appendix B.

3. *Logs.* Each week, you will give the students a log to complete during the week between classes. The students use the logs to record their daily mindfulness practice. The logs also serve as a prompt for developing a sense of gratitude about their lives. In the first class, you will explain how the logs are to be used, and you will emphasize again that it is mandatory for the students to turn in their completed logs in subsequent weeks. You can give some informal feedback during class on what patterns you have noticed with the logs. If you'd like to give the students more structured feedback, you can return the logs to them the following week with your written comments and suggestions. You will find more advice on how to teach the students to use the logs in chapter 6. A copy of the log is provided in appendix C.

> At first, Anne doesn't like the log idea; it just feels like more homework, and she has enough of that! But the teachers have emphasized that it is required, so she completes it on most days of the first week and finds that it helps her stay on track with her meditation homework. At check-in during the second class, she hears several students say how important it was for them to fill in the log; it helped them remember to practice their meditation and also to be more aware of what they have to be grateful for. Anne decides to be more intentional in completing the log during the second week. She chooses showering for her mindful activity and learns how much pleasure a shower can bring. And she finds that filling in the gratitude part of the log forces her to evaluate her day and find something to be grateful for, which in turn seems to improve her mood.

4. *Recorded guided meditations.* Because starting a new meditation practice can be quite challenging, we recommend providing the students with a guided meditation they can use at home. We have produced an audio recording of a brief introduction to mindfulness followed by two guided meditations, one 10 minutes long and the other 20 minutes long. The recording is available on the Duke counseling center's Web site, and we provide CDs for the students during the second class. In our experience, if we give them out during the first class, the students are less likely to go home and practice other skills, so we usually don't offer the recorded meditations until the second class. Students report that the recording is very useful in helping them develop their meditation practice.

> The CD is given out after the second class, and Anne quickly finds that it's one of the things she's grateful for. She likes being guided and also knowing how many minutes the meditation takes. She finds that she can meditate more regularly with the help of the CD.

5. *Music.* Music helps create a peaceful atmosphere; therefore, we recommend playing music quietly while the students are arriving. You should choose music that you enjoy

and find inspiring. We frequently use mood-setting music such as Arvo Part's "Elina" and R. Carlos Nakai's "Canyon Trilogy."

6. *Bell.* We use a small bell to begin and end each meditation. The bell, with its long resonance, provides a lovely beginning and ending to the meditations and helps with the transition into and out of the meditations. You will find a variety of meditation bells available online.

7. *E-mail.* As noted above, we recommend that you send an e-mail before each of the classes. These e-mails serve several functions:

- They remind students about their practice.
- They encourage the students.
- They provide inspiration with quotations from different sources.

We have received much positive feedback on the value of the e-mails. They reinforce our personal connection with our students, helping them to feel free to contact us with questions and concerns.

> Anne tells the teachers at the end of the course that she will miss the e-mails and the logs. She liked the way they encouraged her and gave her structure. She says she always looked forward to the e-mails.

8. *Resource handout.* Your students will need ideas for ways to continue to get support and training in mindfulness once the class is over. We recommend developing a list of local resources that students can refer to as they consider how to maintain their newly acquired skills. Providing this list is one way of helping the students continue their practice after the course is over; we know that it is difficult to maintain a meditation practice alone. See appendix E for an example of the resources we recommend in our "Next Steps" guide.

9. *Written evaluations.* A very important tool for the teachers is the written evaluations you will ask the students to complete at the end of the final class. These have been invaluable to us as we have modified the course over time, working to refine it to better meet the needs of our students. A copy of our evaluation form is presented in appendix F. In chapter 10 we will come back to these evaluations and discuss what they have taught us about the transformation students have experienced in the course.

In the next four chapters, we will review in detail the specifics of each of the four classes. These chapters will clearly outline exactly how to teach each skill and what particular aspect of meditation you will highlight in each class. In addition, you will find frequent questions and comments from the students, as well as our typical responses. These chapters serve as a manual for teachers and should provide all the information you will need to teach Koru.

The First Class

This is my senior year, and I have way too much to do. I can't sleep, and I worry all the time. I'm hoping this class will help me find ways to get through this.

DUKE STUDENT

Most students come to our class because, like the student quoted above, they are struggling with anxiety, worry, and academic or relational stress. This is likely to be true for any group of emerging adults that you are teaching. Often the stress has become so great that it is impairing their ability to perform academically, and they feel a great need for help. At the same time, they may be skeptical about whether the skills you want to teach them can be useful to them, and most have little or no experience with meditation or mindfulness. During the first class, you want the students to begin to experience some relief from the stress and anxiety they are feeling. You also want to familiarize them with the concepts and skills you plan to teach them and help them to develop a willingness to stay open-minded, do the assignments, and see what they observe.

Overview

Each class begins with a brief opening meditation, usually focused on breath awareness. After the opening meditation, you welcome the students and take them through their first *check-in*. In the first class, check-in consists of having the students introduce themselves and articulate their goals and hopes for the class. You will also use the first check-in to introduce yourselves and share your goals for the class.

After check-in and some "housekeeping," you begin the skills-training portion of the class. Two skills are taught during the first class: belly breathing and dynamic breathing. These skills are particularly effective in calming anxiety and are thus a good choice for the first class. Allow time for questions and teaching after the skills training. The final segment of the class, about 15 minutes, is reserved for a guided body-scan meditation.

CHAPTER 6: KEY POINTS

- A brief opening meditation sets the tone of the class.
- Use the initial check-in to have students articulate their goals for the course.
- Introduce and describe mindfulness. Explain to the participants that it requires practice and an open mind.
- Belly breathing, the first skill you teach, is an easily used relaxation skill.
- Dynamic breathing, the second skill taught in this class, works well to reduce high stress/anxiety. Students may be a little skeptical about this skill at first, so encourage them to remain open-minded.
- The body scan is a useful introductory guided meditation.
- The mindfulness log (appendix B) is an important tool for developing a mindfulness practice. Take the time to explain thoroughly how the log is to be used.

Teachings about mindfulness and its benefits are woven in throughout the class. Before the students leave, you introduce their homework assignments and give out the logs they will use to record their required daily meditation practice.

The remainder of this chapter will describe in detail each portion of the first class. We do not use written scripts for our meditations and instructions; however, to help convey the style and language we find most effective, we've included informal scripts. *These will be italicized for your convenience.* We have also included the students' "voices" by quoting both from comments we regularly hear during class and from the evaluations they write at the end of the course. At the end of the chapter, you will find a selection of frequently asked questions and comments with our typical responses.

Getting Started

Before class begins, organize the classroom by moving aside any tables or desks and placing the chairs in a circle. Post a sign on the door that identifies the class and invites late students to enter quietly. The space should be calm and basically quiet, so you may decide, as we have, to have calming music playing in the background as the students come into the room. As the students enter, welcome them and chat informally, perhaps asking about their prior experience, if any, with meditation. Before the class starts, it is a good idea to remind the students to turn off their cell phones and pagers. Also, you should reinforce the calm atmosphere in the room by reducing clutter, so ask the students to place any belongings behind their chairs. There is much to do during the class, so you will want to try to start on time. When the students have settled in, you will lead them through the opening meditation.

Opening Meditation

The brief opening meditation serves two purposes. First, it immediately gives the students an opportunity to relax and to focus their full attention on their present-moment experience, letting go of the pressures and worries that are creating stress for them. Second, it gives the students a brief experience of the concepts you will be discussing throughout the class, which will enhance their learning.

We recommend that you spend about 5 minutes on this meditation, going very slowly and allowing brief periods of silence for the students to practice focusing their attention. We use a bell to begin and end each of our meditation periods. We often allow soft music to continue to play during this time.

The following script captures the basic ideas you want to convey. We have used "..." to suggest places for you to pause briefly before proceeding with the next instruction:

Let's begin by taking just a few minutes to settle into our bodies. Let your feet rest on the floor, back straight, eyes closed or slightly open, gazing toward the floor. Let your hands rest in your lap . . .

[pause]

Let's take a few moments to become aware of our breathing. See if you can find the place in your body where you most easily feel the sensations of your breath. This may be in the rise and fall of your belly, or the rise and fall of your chest, or maybe at the tip of your nose as the air moves in and out . . .

[pause]

Once you've discovered where in your body you can most easily feel your breath, allow your attention to gently settle there as you watch, with curiosity and without judgment, the air moving in and out of your body . . .

[pause]

When your mind starts to wander to thinking about all the work you have to do or whether or not you're going to like this class, or anything else, see if you can just release those thoughts, bringing your attention gently back to the sensations in your body as your breath moves in and out, using your breath as your anchor to your present-moment experience . . .

After the bell has rung for each meditation, we invite the students to raise their arms over their heads for a big stretch as they settle in for the next activity.

Check-in

In this first class, check-in provides you with an opportunity for introductions. As you go around the circle, ask the students to introduce themselves and talk a little bit about what they are hoping to gain from the class. It's helpful if you also state your own goals when you are introducing yourselves; we often say that our goals are to share with the students the meditation skills that have transformed our own lives, as well as to sustain and nurture our own practice. We emphasize that we are part of this learning process. During this first check-in, invite the students to share the quotation from the text that you encouraged them to bring to the first class.

Here are examples of typical goals that students articulate during this first check-in:

- "I'm always thinking about all I have to do, and this makes me really anxious. I want to be more calm."
- "I'm tense all the time, and I just feel so stressed. I'd like to feel less stressed."
- "I tend to worry a lot, and sometimes I can't sleep. I'd like to find a way to just calm down."
- "My time management is terrible, and I just can't concentrate like I used to. It's getting really hard to get my work done. I'm hoping to just get better at focusing and be more effective."
- "I want to be more patient, to learn to 'just be.'"
- "I want to learn new ways to relax."
- "I'm always worrying about what will happen next. I want to learn how to be more in the present."
- "I've heard about meditation and just wanted to learn more about it."

After you've heard from all the students, it's helpful to reflect back to the group what you've heard, emphasizing that the struggles and goals they are bringing to the class are exactly the kinds of issues that mindfulness training can help with. We like to tell the students that they will learn from each other during this class and enrich each other's practice.

At this point in the class, it's time to spend a few minutes covering some of the logistical—or housekeeping—details. Review the schedule and format for the class, reminding the students that you start and end on time, and that if for any reason they can't make the class or will be late, they need to let you know. Ask if the students have acquired the book for the class, *Wherever You Go, There You Are*, and discuss the importance of reading the book to enhance their learning. Talk about your expectation that the students will spend 10 minutes each day practicing one of the mindfulness skills they will be learning and emphasize that it is only through practice that they can experience the benefits of mindfulness. In addition, tell them that although this class is not psychotherapy, what happens in the class is confidential.

Finally, we recommend that you spend a little time introducing the concept of mindfulness and encouraging the students to allow themselves to suspend judgment and develop curiosity. You might start with a quote from Kabat-Zinn's book or another source that seems appropriate to you. This brief discussion usually involves the following information and often includes the metaphor we introduced in chapter 3:

> Mindfulness is simply about learning to pay attention, with an attitude of acceptance, to your present-moment experience. It's simple, very simple, yet not easy at all. As a matter of fact, most students find that when they sit down and try to focus their attention on the sensations in their body, they can only do it for a second or two. This can sometimes lead students to feel that "it's not for me" or that they simply "can't do it." But it's important to understand that although it may be hard at first, that doesn't mean it's impossible. It just means that it's hard. But you guys can all do hard things. I've never met a student here who can't do hard things. You wouldn't be where you are if you couldn't do hard things.
>
> It can be helpful to realize that developing the ability to stay focused in the present without judgment is just a skill that can be learned, like any other skill. For some reason, students tend to think that if they can't do it immediately, then they are incapable of learning it. But really, it's just about training your mind to do something it's not used to doing in the same way you train your bodies. For example, if I asked you to lift a 200-pound weight, you might say you couldn't do it, but you would immediately know a strategy for getting to the place where you could lift 200 pounds. You'd start with smaller weights, and practice every day, and gradually work your way up to the heavier weight.
>
> It's exactly the same with mindfulness practice. We start with small "weights," 10 minutes a day of practicing during periods of relative calm. Gradually, we develop our "mindfulness muscle" and work our way up to heavier and heavier weights. Eventually, we're ready for some heavy lifting, like staying focused and calm when we're trying to study for a test we're worried about, or trying to finish a paper that's almost late, or feeling rejected by someone we really like. Everybody here will have a different "200-pound weight," but I'm sure you each know what it is for you.
>
> So, if you can allow yourself to stay open-minded and curious about this experience and the skills we want to teach you, make a commitment to practice every day for 10 minutes, and suspend your judgment about the process until the end; you will see for yourself what happens. Allow yourself to see what happens as you improve your ability to stay focused, without judgment, on your present-moment experience.

Skills Training: Belly Breathing and Dynamic Breathing

You are now ready to introduce the students to the mindfulness skill for the week. In the first class, you will teach two skills to get the students started. In subsequent classes, you will teach just one skill.

Belly Breathing

This is a fundamental stress-management skill and one that can be used in many situations. We recommend that you follow these steps when teaching belly breathing:

1. *A 2- to 3-minute discussion about breathing.* Discuss how it is both involuntary and under our voluntary control, how it can reflect our mood and also be used to change our mood. Engage the students by asking them if they can suggest what might happen in the body if we breathe more deeply from our belly/diaphragm. You want them to understand the benefits of this type of breathing, such as increased oxygen to the body, decreased heart rate and blood pressure, and stimulation of the immune system.

2. *Finding the diaphragm.* After the students have heard this small discussion, help them find their diaphragm. A helpful exercise is to have them stand up, place their hands on their sides under the rib cage, and make a quick hissing sound. This sound engages the diaphragm, and most students quickly feel their bellies bulging as they hiss. If there are students who cannot feel this, tell them not to worry; it takes practice. This exercise is done in a spirit of fun, and there is often laughter.

3. *Learning to use the belly.* Ask the students to sit and to place one hand on their chest and one on their belly, then close their eyes and breathe normally. Ask them to notice whether their chest or belly rises on inhalation. For those whose bellies don't expand, invite them to make a conscious effort to use their diaphragm when they inhale: *"Push your bellies out consciously when you breathe in as best you can."* We frequently use the phrase "as best you can," and we do not judge or criticize when a skill is difficult for someone. Emphasize that everything takes practice and that the students should try to be compassionate with themselves as they learn.

4. *Practicing.* Ask the students to sit quietly with their eyes closed and to keep practicing, noticing when their mind wanders and coming back over and over to the breath. This is where mindfulness and belly breathing intersect. Counting breaths (to 10 and back, for example) or saying "in" and "out" to oneself can help them focus on their breathing. The room is quiet for a couple of minutes to give the students a chance to practice breathing with mindfulness.

5. *Deeper breathing.* After a few minutes, help the students to deepen and slow down their breathing by inviting them to count silently to three or four on the inhalation and exhalation. Allow them to continue practicing this quietly for a few minutes; then ask them to gently open their eyes.

6. *Feedback.* This first class is on a relatively tight schedule, so we don't allow much time for feedback after teaching this skill. We often wait for feedback until after the second skill has been taught. However, if there is time, ask if anyone wants to reflect on what they've just learned. Almost always, the students report feeling calmer. You might want to mention situations in which they can benefit from this skill—for example, when trying to go to sleep or in any tense situation. We also tell them that this skill is easier to practice while lying flat on the back and invite them to practice this way at home.

Here is what the students say about this skill:

> "Belly breathing [is] most practical, use[d] any time, any place. Love it!"
> "Belly breathing is helpful and a good thing to make a habit of."

Dynamic Breathing (Also Called *Chaotic Breathing*)

The second skill, which has its origins in yoga, may be unfamiliar to you and your students, but it is one of the most popular skills we teach. It is a powerful exercise for immediate tension release and increased energy. There are three components of dynamic breathing. You will model each of them, one at a time, in the following order, asking the students to practice after each step.

1. Breathing quickly but deeply enough through the nose, mouth closed. **It is very important to keep the mouth closed in order to prevent hyperventilation.** This step is done best when sitting on the edge of the seat, with the hands resting on the hips.
2. Using the arms as a bellows to reinforce the breathing: bend the forearms at a 90 degree angle and push the upper arms repeatedly against the sides of the chest in time with the forceful exhalations. The movement is similar to that made by a bird flapping its wings, hence the students' frequent nickname, *chicken breathing.* This step is best done standing.
3. While still standing, adding rhythmic movement in the legs, bending the knees with the exhalations. Tell your students that if this step is too hard to coordinate, it is fine to practice just the first two steps.

This skill looks wild and funny! The students always giggle when we model it. It's helpful to use a lot of humor when introducing this skill to help the students get past their self-consciousness about practicing it in the group. When they themselves are ready to try, we have them stand in a circle with their backs to the center so that they can't see each other. We use fast drumbeat music ("Kundalini" by OSHO) and coach them through 2–3 minutes: *"You can do it! Come on, faster! Remember to keep your mouth closed. Only one minute left! Keep going!"* If anyone feels light-headed, tell them to stop and take deep breaths.

After practicing this skill, have the students return to their seats and ask for their reactions to this skill. The initial responses, besides the laughter, are mostly positive: "I feel less tense." "I feel happier." Some people tell us that they feel tired or light-headed. Emphasize that this skill not only requires practice but also a willingness to stay open and be curious. In the remaining classes, you will hear how students have used and benefited from dynamic breathing. They will report a variety of situations in which they have used it:

- Just before a public presentation
- Late at night, when they need to keep studying but don't have the energy
- When things get tense at work or in a relationship

Of course, doing this skill requires privacy, but we have found that our students can get quite creative about finding places to practice. Some of the funniest moments in our classes have involved students recounting their experience doing "chicken breathing" late at night in library bathrooms or stairwells.

Here is what the students say about this skill:

From an e-mail: "My dad came to stay with me and my husband for a few days. I had to use chaotic breathing to help with the stress! And guess what: my 2-year-old loved watching me, so I didn't have to worry about him wandering off while I closed my eyes. Let other parents in your class know this. I plan to teach my son this exercise when he's older!"

"Thank goodness for dynamic breathing. It's 'unclogged' my mind more than once."

"Dynamic breathing [is] possibly the most useful thing learned at Duke!"

Guided Meditation

The last 15 minutes of class are used to take the students through a guided meditation so that they have the experience of calming their bodies and focusing their minds for a slightly longer period of time. Each week the guided meditation focuses on a different theme. In the first class, you will lead the students through a body scan. What follows is a partial script of the type of body scan we do in class. This particular body scan is based in part on the one used by Jeff Brantley at Duke's Mindfulness-Based Stress Reduction Program. We start and end the meditation by ringing a bell.

In our guided meditation today, we'll be focusing our attention on different body sensations. Today we will use the sensations in our body to help "anchor" our awareness to our present-moment experience. You will find that your mind frequently wanders away from your anchor, which is also known as the "object of meditation." See if you can notice when your mind has wandered, and without making judgments about yourself or your ability to do this, gently bring your attention back to the sensations in your body. It is the nature of the mind to think, and we're not trying to stop the mind from thinking. We're just training the mind to focus better by learning to notice when it has wandered away and gently bringing it back, over and over, to our present-moment experience.

[pause]

Let's again get into our meditation position. Let your feet rest on the floor, hands resting in your lap, eyes closed. See if you can keep your spine straight while your muscles relax around it. Listen for the sound of the bell . . .

[pause]

Let's begin by bringing our awareness to the bottom of our feet as we notice the feeling of our feet resting against the floor. See if you can just notice the sensations in your feet where they rest against the floor . . .

[pause]

Now, as you continue to watch the sensations in your feet, allow yourself also to become aware of your breath moving in and out of your body. See if you can imagine your breath moving in and out through the bottom of your feet . . .

[pause]

With each inhalation, allow your awareness to sharpen; with each exhalation, allow tension and tightness to be released from your feet. Breathing in, focus your attention; breathing out, release tension . . .

[pause]

(Allow a brief period of silence before moving to the next body part, to allow the students a chance to practice focusing their attention.)

Now, move your awareness up to the muscles of your calves. And as you allow your attention to settle there, begin to imagine your breath moving in and out through your calf muscles, noting carefully the sensations in the calves . . .

[pause]

You might notice tightness or tingling, the feeling of air or your clothes against your skin, or perhaps nothing at all. See if you can just be aware of whatever is there. And with each inhalation, sharpen your focus on the sensations; with each exhalation, release tightness and tension . . .

[pause]

If your mind wanders, see if you can just notice that, and with an attitude of kindness and patience, bring your attention back to the sensations in your calves.

The body scan continues in this way as you move up the body. Adjusting as needed for the amount of time available, you will usually focus on the thighs, hands, belly, arms, back, shoulders and neck, jaws, muscles around the eyes, and the forehead. This meditation can be lengthened by adding more parts of the body or done fairly briefly by just picking a few. Typically, we end it in the following way:

Now let's take a few moments to slowly scan our awareness through our body from head to toe. If you notice any areas of tightness or tension, let your awareness settle there for a few moments, breathing in and out through that tight place, and observing the sensations there. And again, when you notice that your mind has wandered, gently bring it back to the sensations in your body . . .

[pause]

When you hear the sound of the bell, make a commitment to bring this level of awareness to all of your activities for the rest of the day.

After the bell has rung we say, *"and stretch,"* as we again stretch our arms over our heads for a moment.

Closing Instructions and Comments

At the end of the first class, you will pass out the syllabus (appendix B) and the logs (appendix C). You will then give the students instructions on how to use the logs. The logs have a table to record on a daily basis the mindfulness exercise they have practiced and how many minutes they practiced. Remind the students that they can practice mindful breathing, belly breathing, dynamic breathing, or a body scan for their required 10 minutes of daily practice.

The logs also have a space at the top to identify one *daily-life* activity that the students will practice doing mindfully each day, such as brushing their teeth or walking to class. Explain that the point of all the mindfulness training is not that they become highly trained meditators, but rather that they develop the habit of bringing mindfulness into their day-to-day activities on a regular basis. To encourage this habit, they are asked to identify one activity that they do each day and make that their daily-life mindfulness activity. You might suggest options such as brushing their teeth, washing their face, climbing into bed, walking to class, or showering. Once they have selected the activity, the goal is to perform that activity with intense present-moment awareness as much as possible throughout the week.

The final element of the log is the *gratitude record*. There is space on the log for the students to record each day two things they are grateful for in their lives. Let them know that gratitude is an important mindfulness practice, as it allows them to bring into their daily awareness people, events, or sensations that make their lives rich and pleasurable. Left to their own devices, our minds tend to gravitate toward problems or worries. By intentionally bringing our awareness to aspects of our lives that give us pleasure, we can improve our mood and decrease our stress. Emphasize that it is fine to chart anything they feel grateful for, be it unusual or mundane; it's okay to be grateful for the same two things every day. What's important is the act of intentionally bringing awareness to something in your life that you recognize as pleasant or meaningful.

As the students are leaving, invite them to try to continue their body awareness as they depart, noticing how it feels to rise from their chairs and walk down the stairs and into the fresh evening air. Encourage them to notice the sensations, thoughts, and feelings that arise as they return to the busy-ness of their lives.

When the last student has left, take the time to sit for a few moments to review what has happened in the class. Invariably, after each class we are inspired—as you will be—by the openness and willingness we have witnessed. We know that transformation has already begun for most of the students, and we eagerly look forward to seeing them the following week.

Frequently Asked Questions

The following is a list of our responses to the questions and comments we commonly hear from students during the first class, either at check-in or while processing their new skills. We find that we hear the same questions over and over, reflecting the similarity of the struggles that students face when they take on this unfamiliar practice.

Q: What's the difference between *mindfulness* and *meditation*?

A: *This is an important question, and one we are asked all the time. As we've said, mindfulness is about paying attention, with an attitude of curiosity and acceptance, to whatever it is that you're doing. You can bring mindfulness to anything you do: walking to class, doing your work, talking to a friend, brushing your teeth. And the more time you spend being mindful, the less stressed you will feel. So, mindfulness is something you can experience anytime.*

Meditation is one of the ways we learn to be mindful, and formal meditation time is one of the best ways to build your "mindfulness muscle" so that you can be more present as you go about your day. So, when we talk about meditation, we're talking about the times when you set the intention to spend a period of time bringing your attention back, over and over again, to your present-moment experience. In this way, the skills that you learn in this class and the guided meditations we do are all "meditations" that will improve your ability to stay mindful at other times.

Q: The belly breathing felt relaxing, but I had a hard time staying awake.

A: *Students often find that they fall asleep when they sit down to belly breathe and start feeling relaxed. Part of the problem is that you guys are all sleep-deprived, and as soon as you slow down for a minute, it's natural that you fall asleep. You probably need some sleep. That's something to be aware of and consider: if finding ways to get more regular sleep would help you to feel better in general.*

So, there's nothing wrong with falling asleep. As a matter of fact, doing some belly breathing is a great way to clear your mind and relax your body at night to help you get to sleep.

But it's true that sleeping isn't meditating, so there are a few tricks for working with sleepiness. First, it's important not to judge yourself for feeling sleepy. It's just sleepiness! No big deal. Second, see if you can become a little bit curious about how it feels to be sleepy. How do you know you're sleepy? What are the sensations in your body and mind that tell you you're sleepy? Sometimes just being curious about sleepiness can make you feel more alert. You can also try opening your eyes while you continue to practice breathing. Some people recommend standing up or gently pinching your earlobes when you begin to feel sleepy.

If these tricks don't help, it may be best to try a more energizing meditation, such as dynamic breathing, which we've just learned, or walking meditation, which we'll learn next week.

Q: What's the best time of day to practice?

A: *Anytime that you can get yourself to do it is the best time! It doesn't matter when this happens; just do it! What matters is that you practice regularly so that you have a chance to develop your skills and to see if the practice helps you meet the goals you articulated at the start of class today. Be willing to experiment a little. Pick a time to do your 10 minutes of practice, and if after a few days you find that it's not working well for you, then see if there's another time that would work better. Just see if you can stay committed to really trying for the next 4 weeks so that you have a chance to determine if this practice can make a difference for you.*

Q: I'm already so busy. I don't see how I can make time to meditate. I'm feeling more stressed just thinking about adding something else to my schedule.

A. *I know. You guys are so busy that it can be hard to come up with 10 minutes. But see if there's some time in your day, maybe when you need a break at the library, or after you turn your computer off for the night, or before you go to class, when you can set aside 10 minutes to practice your skills. Most students find that if they pick a specific time and plan to practice at that time every day, they do a better job of sticking with it. Sometimes it's helpful to have a timer or set your cell phone as a reminder.*

Q: Is dynamic breathing really meditation? How can it relax you if it increases your heart rate?

A: *Remember that mindfulness and meditation are not necessarily about feeling relaxed. They're just about paying attention, with an attitude of acceptance, to what you are experiencing in this moment, whatever that may be. Dynamic breathing is a good way to clear your mind and focus on the present. As a matter of fact, it's hard to think of anything else when you're fully engaged in dynamic breathing. How many of you found your mind wandering during the dynamic breathing exercise? So, using dynamic breathing to focus your mind when you are stressed or really tired is very useful.*

Q: I'm not sure I agree with this whole "acceptance" idea. It seems to me that going around accepting all your problems without trying to do anything about them doesn't make sense.

A: *Yes, "acceptance" can be a tricky word, and it's important to understand that we don't mean "passive resignation." This practice is not about being passive in the face of problems; as a matter of fact, the kind of acceptance we're talking about should improve your ability to problem-solve.*

When we talk about acceptance, we mean simply seeing clearly how things really are in this moment—not how you wish things are or how you think they should be, but how they really are. You will find that once you can see clearly how things really are, you'll be in a much better position to decide, with wisdom, how to act. For example, if you're a grad student and you're working in a lab with an adviser who is more harmful than helpful to you, you won't be able to change your situation until you see clearly what the problems are and what your options are. Sometimes when we clearly see our situation, we understand that the wisest choice is to wait with patience before acting; at other times, we know that the wisest choice is to act mindfully to change the situation. So, acceptance is really about seeing clearly and acting wisely. The moment you bring your full attention to the present moment, you are practicing acceptance of that very moment. (See chapter 3 for other ideas about how to talk to students about acceptance.)

The Second Class

When the second class begins, the students have had 1 week of practice with their mindfulness skills. Most have done at least some of the reading, so they are now becoming familiar with the concepts and have some sense of the potential the practice offers. You will likely be impressed by the positive changes they are already reporting. At the same time, they have probably experienced some frustration as they set about trying to focus their minds and stay present. Generally, some students will feel discouraged, whereas others will feel enthused. During this second class, it's important for you to work with the obstacles the students may describe as a way helping them stay engaged in continuing to practice. We find that the first 2 weeks are the trickiest for the students, and it's helpful to support them with a lot of problem solving, humor, and optimism.

Overview

You should collect the students' meditation logs as they arrive at the class. One of the teachers can look over the logs as they are handed in and make a few general comments about them at some point. If you would like to give the students more formal feedback on the logs, you can return them in the next class with your written comments.

The second class begins with an opening meditation and check-in. During check-in, encourage the students to talk about their experiences while practicing their mindfulness skills over the previous week. You should use the students' responses as indicators of where they are with the practice and focus your teaching accordingly. In this class, the students often have many questions and need a lot of support, so check-in takes a large amount of class time.

The mindfulness skill taught in the second class is walking meditation. We used to teach walking meditation in the fourth class, but our students repeatedly told us they needed to learn this skill sooner. This need probably reflects the students' restlessness or fatigue, which deters them from being effectively focused when they are sitting still.

CHAPTER 7: KEY POINTS

- Collect the logs when the students enter the class to emphasize that they are expected to do their mindfulness homework.
- Check-in provides the first opportunity to hear about the students' practice. Use their comments as prompts for your teaching.
- Today's skill, walking meditation, is a good way for restless or sleepy students to practice meditation.
- Gathas, which are meditation poems, help students anchor their attention in the present moment during sitting meditation.

The guided meditation for this class involves teaching the students a *gatha*, or meditation poem, that they can use to help anchor their thoughts a little more firmly. Many students report that the gatha is the most useful aid for their sitting meditations.

Opening Meditation

Since the students are now familiar with the schedule, you can start immediately with the opening meditation. Here's a sample of a typical opening meditation for the second class. Pause for 15–20 seconds between each instruction, planning to spend about 5 minutes on this meditation. If you like, you can begin and end the session by ringing a bell.

Let's get into our meditation positions, feet on the floor, backs straight, hands resting in your lap. Begin by checking in with your body for a few moments, noticing without judging how you feel physically and emotionally . . .

[pause]

Now move your awareness to your breath as you begin to watch that one place where you can most easily feel your breath as it gently moves in and out of your body. Allow your breath to be natural, not forced or pressured . . .

[pause]

You will probably notice many thoughts arising about what you've been doing or what you need to do. See if you can just let those thoughts go as you settle into this space, allowing your awareness of the present moment to open. Releasing judgments and plans and worries . . .

[pause]

Calming your body and your mind as you return your attention again and again to your breath, your anchor to your present-moment experience . . .

[Pause, then gently ring your bell or chime.]

And as you open your eyes, stretch . . .

[pause]

(Invite the students to join you as you stretch your arms up over your head.)

Check-in

The first opportunity for you to learn how well the students are doing with their new practice comes during check-in of the second class. During this check-in, we recommend that you ask each student to share his or her experiences with the daily mindfulness practice over the past week. It is a good idea to go systematically around the room so that everyone gets a chance to say something. You can also take the roll at the same time and continue learning everyone's name. At the end of the chapter, you'll find a list of questions students often have during the second class. Here's a sample of typical comments from the students during the check-in of the second class:

- "I had a very stressful week. I used belly breathing and dynamic breathing, and I think they really helped."
- "I was in the library trying to study but not getting anything done, so I went into the bathroom and did the chicken dance [dynamic breathing]. It felt stupid but it helped clear my mind."
- "I'm feeling frustrated and restless when I try to meditate. It's a struggle—I sometimes feel like there's no point in trying."
- "The book is helping me understand that I'm not supposed to just be relaxing myself."
- "I'm noticing how judgmental I am and feeling really frustrated about that."
- "I liked writing down what I was grateful for, but it was hard for me to remember to stay mindful of the daily-life activity every day."

After the check-in, it's helpful to summarize the themes that the students have touched on. Reading an excerpt from *Wherever You Go, There You Are* that highlights one of the themes is a useful way to tie the required readings to the class teachings. Another option is to read a script that illustrates the way the mind wanders when we attempt to focus our attention. Students can usually identify with this and find it funny. Here's the script we use (but you could make up your own):

> Breathing. Breathing . . . [pause]I wonder if I'm doing this right . . . breathing . . .
> I can't do this! Oh, I'm not supposed to judge. . . . . Breathing . . . breathing. . . .
> I have to get that paper done tonight! I can't believe I waited until the last minute again.
> . . . . Oh, back to the breath. . . . Wonder what I'll do for dinner. . . . Breathing. . . . .
> Breathing. . . . This isn't so hard. Oh, I'm thinking again. I'll NEVER get this right!

Skills Training: Walking Meditation

Walking meditation is an important meditation to use when people are too restless or anxious to sit still. It is also useful for students who find that they fall asleep when they try to do sitting meditation. In walking meditation the sensation of the feet contacting the floor, rather than breath sensations, is the primary focus. Some students find this a much more tangible anchor for their awareness and feel that it helps them to focus better.

Ideally, walking meditation should be taught with the students lined up down the length of the room, with each student walking his or her own path, at his or her own pace across the room. If, like us, you do not have a room large enough to allow this, it is possible to teach this skill with the students walking in a circle.

Begin by asking the students to mindfully place their chairs in the center of the room, and then invite them to stand in a circle around the chairs, facing the center. Once the students are ready, you can instruct them as follows:

> This new kind of meditation is a movement meditation and can be handy
> when you feel too restless or too sleepy to sit for your meditation practice.
> In this case, our attention is on our feet; our mindfulness of the sensations in
> our feet as we walk anchors us in the present moment, just as the breath does
> when we practice sitting meditation. Our walking is very slow; you have
> probably never walked this slowly. Be careful, and if you find that you are
> losing your balance, then adjust by walking faster, stepping outside of the
> circle if you need to. Many people enjoy walking barefoot, so please feel free
> to take off your shoes.
>
> As always, we will notice how our thinking mind wants to be active. We will
> find ourselves lost in thought over and over; and over and over we will bring our
> attention back, with gentleness and compassion, to the sensations in our feet. We
> may also notice thoughts of judging such as "I don't like this" or "I'm doing this
> wrong" or "Boy, this is way too slow for me." So, again, we notice the judging and
> return to our awareness practice.

The following instructions are for guiding the students to walk together in a circle. If you have room for them to spread out and each walk his or her own path, all the better, but you will need to adapt the instructions slightly. Remember to speak slowly, allowing time between each step for the students to practice each instruction.

1. *Place your feet solidly beneath you in line with your shoulders, arms hanging comfortably at your side. Now close your eyes and let yourself feel what it is like to stand, feeling the floor beneath your feet.*

2. *Now, with eyes open or closed, gently and slowly lift your right heel off the floor, keeping the ball of your foot on the floor. Notice what this feels like; now place your heel back on the floor. Do the same with your left foot.*

3. *Now try walking in place, keeping your attention on the soles of your feet and noticing all the movements that are a part of walking.*

4. *Open your eyes and turn to the right. Your eyes should be on the floor in front of you, not on the person in front of you.*

5. *I will set the pace. With the right foot first, begin to walk slowly, lifting the heel of your right foot, then your toes, lifting your foot and moving it slowly forward. Shift your weight forward as you place your right foot on the ground and the heel of your left foot begins to lift.*

6. *Allow your attention to remain focused on the sensations in your feet as you slowly move forward, shifting your weight, lifting and placing your feet with full awareness.*

Once the students have started walking, they walk mostly in silence, although on occasion you may remind them to bring their awareness back to the movements of their feet. After about 5 minutes, ask the students to pause, then slowly and mindfully turn and face the opposite direction, carefully watching the shifting of their weight on their feet as they turn. Then invite them to begin walking again. If you have enough time, allow them to walk in silence for another few minutes. In the last minute or so, you can invite them walk at a faster pace so that they can experience maintaining awareness of walking at a more normal speed.

When this meditation is over, have the students mindfully return their chairs to their former positions and ask them for feedback. Usually some students report that they found it easier to focus their awareness during walking meditation compared to sitting meditation, whereas others report that it was harder. You can encourage them to practice this new skill over the next week, and often you will hear in subsequent classes that they have practiced walking meditation and found it useful.

This is what the students say about this skill:

"Awesome for anxiety!"
"Great when I'm stressed!"

Guided Meditation: Gathas

The guided meditation for the second class is used to teach the students a gatha, or meditation poem. The purpose of the gatha is to strengthen the students' focus on their breath when they are trying to do a sitting meditation. You will teach the students to link the words of the gatha to their breathing, repeating them silently to themselves as they watch their breath. Linking words to the breath in this way provides a "heavier" anchor for the students, and they find that they can maintain their present-moment awareness more consistently.

The gatha we use is adapted from one by Thich Nhat Hanh, a well-known and well-loved meditation teacher. It is reprinted from *Being Peace* (1987, p. 5) by Thich Nhat Hanh with permission of Parallax Press, Berkeley, California. www.parallax.org.

I know I am breathing in	IN
I know I am breathing out	OUT
Breathing in, I calm my body	CALMING
Breathing out, I smile	SMILING
I dwell in the present moment	PRESENT MOMENT
I know this is a precious moment	PRECIOUS MOMENT

Hand out copies of the gatha to the students and read aloud to them the verse written on the left side of the page. As you begin the meditation, you will slowly repeat the lines of the gatha, trying to time them to the flow of breath. As the meditation proceeds, you will instruct the students to shorten their internal "chant" to just the one or two words written in capital letters on the right side of the page. Tell the students that they will "say" the words silently in their minds, linking them to an in or out breath so that the words are repeated over and over, following the rhythm of the breath.

The students are often a little suspicious of this practice when it is first introduced. The whole calming, smiling, precious moment thing can seem a little too touchy-feely for them. You will need to encourage them to keep an open mind and try it. There are always a number of students who really like it and a few students who report that it is the most useful practice for them.

You can introduce the gatha in the following way:

For our guided meditation today, we're going to teach you a gatha, or meditation poem. The purpose of the gatha is to give you some assistance in keeping your mind focused on your breath. We talked earlier today about our minds being rivers of rushing thoughts [see "Frequently Asked Questions" below]. You can think of using a gatha as a way of putting a ladder or rope on the bank of your "river," making it a little easier to climb out each time.

You'll notice, as you start to pay attention to your thinking, that there are two different "states" of mind. We can call them "thinking mind" and "observing mind." We spend the vast majority of time locked in thinking mind. Thinking mind is working when we are planning, judging, evaluating, or worrying.

With mindfulness we're trying to develop the strength of observing mind. Observing mind is working when we become aware of sensations, thoughts, and feelings as they arise in the present moment. Observing mind allows present-moment awareness and some distance from the worries, plans, and judgments of thinking mind. The problem is, since we use thinking mind so much more often, it's initially much more powerful than observing mind. And when you try to switch to observing mind, thinking mind comes barreling in, taking over all the action. Thinking mind can be a bit like an active puppy, running from place to place, never staying still. Gathas are tools that we use to give thinking mind something to do so that observing mind has a chance to take hold and perhaps grow a little stronger. It's like tossing a bone to your active puppy, which causes the puppy to stop and settle in one place. It's much easier to calmly observe the puppy once it is quiet and still.

Now let me warn you that when I first introduce the gatha, you may notice yourself feeling skeptical about it. See if you can just observe that attitude, remain open-minded, and notice what happens when you use it. We usually hear that students find the gatha to be very helpful.

I will lead you through a meditation using a gatha, but let me explain a little bit about how it will work. We will begin by repeating silently to ourselves the lines of the gatha written on the left side of the page I've just given you. As you meditate, link the phrases to your breath so that each line corresponds to an in breath or an out breath. After a few breaths, we will focus more deeply by dropping all the words of the gatha except for the ones written in capital letters on the right side of the page. I know this may sound a little confusing, but as I lead you through it, it will become more clear.

One other thing: when you get to the line "I smile" or "SMILING," see what happens if you actually put a smile on your face at that moment. Just notice anything that happens in your body when you smile. Now, let's put the papers with the gatha written on it away and get into our meditation positions.

We use the bell to signal the beginning and end of the meditation, allowing about 15 minutes to complete the exercise. The guided meditation usually goes something like this:

Relax into your chair, feet on the floor, hands resting in your laps, backs straight, eyes closed. Allow your awareness to settle on your breath for a few moments. As you continue to watch your breath, begin to link the lines of the gatha to your breathing.

I know I am breathing in. I know I am breathing out. Breathing in, I calm my body. Breathing out, I smile. I dwell in the present moment. I know this is a precious moment . . .

(Repeat this two or three times before going on to the next instruction.)

[pause]

> *Now let's drop down to just one word, keeping it linked with our breath.*
> *In . . . out . . . calming . . . smiling . . . present moment . . . precious moment . . .*
> *in . . . out . . . calming . . . smiling . . . present moment . . . precious moment . . .*

(Repeat this slowly two or three times, trying to time your words to the rhythm of the breath, then pause for a minute or so to let the students practice on their own.)

[pause]

Notice what happens in your body and to your feelings when you smile . . .

[pause]

If your mind wanders, come back to your breath and your words. In . . . out . . . calming . . . smiling . . . present moment . . . precious moment . . .

[pause]

(Allow the students to practice in silence for a few minutes. With about 3–5 minutes left in the meditation, proceed with the rest of the script.)

> *Now, if you're feeling that your concentration has stabilized a bit, you can try releasing the words and letting your awareness settle again on the sensations of your breath. If your mind gets too restless, you can always go back to your gatha.*

(End with several minutes of silence before ringing the bell.)
This is what students say about this skill:

"I think [the most meaningful part of the class] was learning to concentrate on my breath as an 'anchor' to the present moment, especially with the gatha we learned."
"I liked using the gatha with belly breathing to keep me focused."

Closing Comments

After the meditation, pass out the new logs for the next week. This is usually the time when we offer the students our audio recording of guided meditations with which to practice. We have a CD to give the students, or they can download it from our Web site. Remind the students that for this week's homework they can use the skills they learned last week or try walking meditation, practice with their gatha, or use the recorded guided meditations. As they leave, consider encouraging them to continue keeping their awareness in the present moment as they gather their things, walk outside, and step out into the beauty of the day.

Frequently Asked Questions

Some of these questions will come up during check-in, others after the students have practiced a skill. Each one provides a great opportunity for teaching.

Q: I'm still not clear about what the goal is supposed to be when I'm trying to meditate.

A: *One of the enjoyable but confusing things about learning mindfulness is getting comfortable with all the paradoxes. One thing we learn is that in this practice the harder we strive for a particular outcome, the less likely it is to occur. For example, if you sit down to meditate determined to create a particular state of relaxation, and you get all wound up and determined to MAKE it happen, it's not likely to happen. The paradox is this: the more you are willing to open to the moment and accept things as they are without being too attached to the idea of relaxing, the more likely it is that you will experience the benefits of feeling focused and relaxed. So, you can get what you want, but only if you don't try to get what you want. Confusing, yes?*

The problem is, though, that most people will not go to the trouble of meditating if they don't have some goal they are trying to accomplish, like the ones you mentioned last week: trying to decrease stress, improve sleep, and improve concentration. That's why you are all here learning this new practice. One helpful way to think about it is to keep your goals in mind as you are making the time and preparing to practice. However, as soon as you sit down to breathe or start your walking meditation, try to let go of the goals and just practice staying present, accepting whatever arises.

Q: What arises for me is a lot of thoughts. It's so frustrating that I can't get my thoughts to stop.

A: *Remember, we're not trying to get our thoughts to stop. Our thoughts never stop. Brains produce thoughts. That's just the way it is.*

It can be useful to think of your mind as a rushing river. There are always thoughts rushing along in a torrent. With mindfulness practice, we're not trying to stop the river, we're just trying to climb out of the river; we're trying to settle in on the bank for a moment so that we can watch the thoughts go by. You'll see, as you start to work with staying present and becoming aware of your thoughts, that it feels very different to be in the river carried away by the thoughts versus sitting on the bank watching them go by. So, with the meditations and skills we're teaching, we're just trying to help you learn to climb out of the river. Of course, you fall back in almost immediately. That's how it works: climb out, fall in, climb out, fall in. But after a while, you'll notice that you can stay on the bank for longer periods of time. And eventually, you'll notice that the river sometimes slows down quite a bit, but, of course, only if you're not trying to make it slow down!

Q: I feel so restless. Ten minutes can seem like an eternity. What should I do?

A: *It's typical for students who are first trying to meditate to feel either very sleepy or very restless. We talked a little bit about sleepiness last time, so let's talk about restlessness now. It can be really hard to sit with restlessness, but it can be a great teacher, too. If you're feeling restless, then you probably will feel more comfortable trying one of the moving meditations like dynamic breathing or walking meditation. There's absolutely nothing wrong with using those skills for your mindfulness practice.*

On the other hand, trying to sit with your restlessness, without judging it, even for a few minutes, can be instructive. Here's why: often we have to do something that we don't enjoy or that is not comfortable, like writing a long paper at night when we'd rather be sleeping or partying. If you start to pay attention, you'll begin to notice that the more you fight and resist doing something you don't like, the more painful it becomes and the more you suffer. The longer you spend fretting and agonizing about writing the paper, the longer it takes and the more miserable you feel. But if you can just accept that you have to write the paper and it doesn't feel that great, but nothing bad is happening and it won't last forever, the easier it gets to just relax and do it.

Working with restlessness in meditation is a great way to practice working with things we don't like, learning that we can manage those uncomfortable feelings without anything bad happening and learning that the feelings always go away. They never last forever. So, if you're sitting down to watch your breath for a few minutes and you start feeling restless, see if you can relax into it. Notice what it feels like in your body. How do your body and mind know that you're restless? If you just sit and breathe deeply, not judging the feeling but being interested in it, what happens? Does it get stronger? Does it get weaker? Does it change more with the in breath or more with the out breath? Is it uncomfortable? If so, where in your body do you feel it?

If you learn to sit with restlessness, you will also learn how to tolerate more easily other difficult situations and emotions in your life. And of course, the paradox is at work again: when you cease to view the restlessness as a problem, it will go away.

Q: What should I do if I have an itch?

A: *Scratch it! But, try to wait a few seconds before you do so. It can be interesting to notice for just a few seconds what happens to the itch and your thoughts about the itch if you don't immediately scratch it. Again, we can learn a lot by getting familiar with the way our mind reacts when we're uncomfortable. If you don't scratch the itch, and watch it with patience instead of fighting it, you'll probably notice that it goes away of its own accord. Another life lesson: all of our uncomfortable feelings will change and go away over time, even if we don't "do" something about them.*

Q: I had a hard time remembering to do my daily-life mindfulness activity. I picked brushing my teeth but didn't remember to do it even once.

A: *Remembering to do the daily-life exercise is probably hard for all of you. How many of you had trouble remembering to do your activity? See, it's most of the group. The point of this activity is to help you begin to develop the habit of being mindful during some of the ordinary moments in your life. But it's hard to break the habit of being mindless, on automatic pilot, the way we usually are when we go about our daily tasks. Most of us will need reminders of some sort. Since you've picked brushing your teeth, you might try putting a sticky note in a strategic place to remind you, like on your tube of toothpaste. Setting an alarm in your phone can be helpful as well. If you are filling in your log each evening, something as simple as highlighting the daily-life activity can draw your attention to it. You can also try picking a different activity if your first one doesn't work out for you. Get creative and experiment with different ideas until you find something that works.*

Q: I started the week really well, doing my meditation every day. But then I was bad and didn't do it the last few days. I just got busy and forgot about it.

A: *First, notice the judgment. Were you really "bad" because you forgot to meditate? Probably not. See if you can notice when you have those kinds of judging thoughts about yourself or others.*

Now, in trying to practice your meditation more regularly, it may be helpful to designate a specific time each day for it. It's tricky for students, because your schedules tend to be different every day. You'll get up for an early class one day, then sleep in until your afternoon class the next. That kind of irregularity makes it hard, but not impossible, to work meditation consistently into your day. Try setting your phone alarm to go off at a certain time each day to remind you. Or put a sticky note on your computer to remind you to spend 10 minutes watching your breath when you open it. Or put your meditation log by your bed to remind you to meditate before you go to sleep or when you wake up in the morning. If you just count on remembering and working it in at different times each day, you are much less likely to practice consistently.

Q: I notice a lot of judging thoughts. It's frustrating to me, and I don't know what to do about it.

A: *It may help you to know that you don't need to do anything about the judging thoughts. Just notice that you're having them. As you begin to notice them without fighting them, your relationship to those thoughts will change. And that's when they start to go away. If you try to order your mind to stop judging, it will just judge more.*

Developing this attitude is critical to the practice of mindfulness: Being willing to let things be as they are—if you're judging, you're judging; no big deal. Letting go of an agenda and not striving all the time to make things different. Cultivating feelings of patience and kindness. All of these attitudes will contribute to your sense of well-being as you increasingly keep your attention focused on the present moment. As we talked about last week, seeing things as they are and being willing to accept each moment as it is does not mean living a life of passive resignation. It is only by clearly seeing each moment as it is that we develop balance and wisdom, which then lead to effective actions that can result in positive change.

Q: I was up late trying to write a paper last week, and I felt myself getting so stressed out. I did that fast-breathing exercise and it helped, but I still couldn't get the work done, which made me even more stressed. I'm not sure what to do about that.

A: *This is a situation in which mindfulness can be very useful. I'm guessing that if you are sitting in front of the computer feeling stressed out, you are probably having all sorts of thoughts that aren't useful: "I hate this. I'll never get it done. I should have started sooner. I can't believe I'm so stupid. This is so lousy. I'm probably going to fail this class; then my entire future will go down the tubes." We often hear this kind of catastrophic thinking from students, and it's understandable. But what would happen if you shifted you attention fully into awareness of your present-moment physical sensations. Likely, what is actually happening in the present moment is that you are sitting in a comfortable chair, in a room that is at a comfortable temperature, and you can feel your fingers tapping on the keyboard. Probably nothing bad or even physically uncomfortable is happening to you. If you can keep your thinking mind simply on the topic at hand, rather than on all the judging thoughts, your creativity is likely to start flowing. If you can notice and let go of the worries and judgments, focusing instead on what is going on in the moment, you will notice your stress level dropping. But don't just take my word for it. Give it a try next time you are completing an assignment. Let us know what happens.*

Q: I've been practicing being mindful when I walk my dog and listen to my iPod. Is that meditating?

A: *As we talked about last week, there is a difference between formal meditation and mindfully doing any activity. You can be mindful doing absolutely anything. However, if you want to develop the ability to really stay present and calm in difficult situations, you will need to do some formal meditation practice. And that means setting aside time, preferably in silence, to practice bringing your mind back, over and over again, to your object of meditation, which may be your breath or the sensations in your feet during walking meditation. It's great to have a wonderful, mindful walk with your dog while listening to great music. I highly recommend that you keep doing this. But if you want to build your mindfulness muscle, you will also need to spend some time in formal meditation practice.*

Q: Can I lie down to meditate?

A: *Of course. But if you're like most students, you'll immediately fall asleep. If you are meditating in the evening in order to calm your mind and relax your body to help you sleep, it can be very useful to meditate lying down.*

Q: Am I supposed to be focusing on my breath during the walking meditation? Am I supposed to match my steps to my breath?

A: *In the walking meditation, the object of meditation is not generally your breath. It is instead the sensations in your feet as you walk. You may notice your breath, and perhaps notice that it is matched to your stride, but you don't have to do this. In this practice, you're using the sensations in your feet as your anchor to the present moment. When you notice that your mind has wandered, just bring it gently back, with kindness and acceptance, to awareness of the sensations in your feet. Some people find that it is much easier for them to feel and focus on the sensations in their feet during a walking meditation than it is to feel and focus on their breath during a sitting meditation.*

The Third Class

By the time the third class begins, the students have been practicing mindfulness and meditation for 2 to 3 weeks (often there is a spring or fall break between the second and third classes). Many of them are starting to see the benefits of their practice. During check-in, you will likely begin to hear stories about transformation and questions about the significance of different experiences. At the same time, there are always a few students who are still struggling and perhaps feeling discouraged. During this class, you can help by supporting the students who feel they are making progress and by continuing to actively guide and encourage those who are struggling.

Overview

The third class follows the format of the second class. The class begins by collecting the meditation logs as the students come in; you may offer comments or have brief discussions with students as they turn in their logs. You will begin with an opening meditation and move to check-in, where this week you are likely to hear stories of success and struggle. Students often have questions about problems that have arisen as they practice.

The stress-management skill taught in the third class is guided imagery. Students are led through a visualization exercise and taught how to generate these visualizations on their own. Generally, students find that this skill can enhance their ability to relax.

The guided meditation for the third class focuses on working with thoughts. Students have the most questions and the most difficulty dealing with the rush of thoughts produced by their stressed-out minds, so we find it helpful to give them extra practice in working with their thoughts.

Opening Meditation

Here is a suggested script for the opening meditation for this class. Pause for 20 seconds or more between each phrase, allowing the meditation to last for about 5 minutes. If you like, open and close the meditation by ringing a bell.

CHAPTER 8: KEY POINTS

- By the third class, students are beginning to experience the benefits of their daily mindfulness practice. Their questions and comments reflect their growing understanding of the underlying concepts.
- Guided imagery, the skill taught in this class, helps students develop deeper levels of calm relaxation.
- Labeling thoughts during meditation helps develop observing mind and trains students to work with thoughts that arise during meditation.
- Remind the students that they have just 1 more week to practice their skills before the course ends. This can help them maintain their motivation to keep practicing.

Welcome, everyone. Let's get into our meditation positions—feet on the floor in front of you, back straight but not rigid, hands resting comfortably in your laps. Gently close your eyes . . .

[pause]

Take a couple of big sighs to let go of the tensions and worries you brought into the room today and to come more fully into this moment. Check in with your body, noticing how you are feeling right now . . .

[pause]

Now bring your focus, your awareness, to your breath, wherever you feel it most comfortably . . .

[pause]

Shine the light of your awareness on your breath . . .

[pause]

When your thoughts wander, bring your awareness gently and with compassion back to your breath. Remember: this is a practice of gentleness and compassion . . .

If we have to come back to the breath a hundred times, we come back a hundred times . . .

[pause]

And now gently, when you are ready, open your eyes.

Check-in

You will begin check-in by asking the students to share their experience, their successes and challenges, with their meditation practice over the preceding weeks. The comments and questions start to get a bit more complex by the third week as the students deepen their mindfulness practice. The "Frequently Asked Questions" section at the end of the chapter reflects typical questions raised during check-in of the third class. Here are some typical comments:

- "I thought the CD was really helpful. I need someone guiding me in meditation."
- "I wanted to try walking meditation, but I live in a dorm room and there's no space and someone is always there."
- "I've been bad this week. I had too much to do to meditate."
- "Such a wonderful thing happened to me. I tried being mindful in Duke Gardens yesterday, and it was just awesome!"
- "I still like belly breathing best. I do it for my meditation every day."
- "I used walking to class as my everyday mindfulness activity this week. I didn't remember it every day, but when I did, I felt much less stressed."

Again, check-in will prompt much of the direct teaching in this class as you respond to the students' questions and concerns. Once all of the students have had a chance to share, you may choose to read a quote from Kabat-Zinn's book *Wherever You Go, There You Are* (1994) before moving on to skills training.

Skills Training: Guided Imagery

Introduce this skill by telling the students that guided imagery is a means "to calm yourself, to change your mood, to take a vacation in your mind." You may want to tell them that there are other ways to use guided imagery, such as visualizing a specific desired outcome (e.g., walking across the stage to get your diploma at graduation). Guided imagery can also be used to support healing, as when cancer patients imagine their immune system's cells attacking their cancer cells.

The most important part of imaging, you should tell the class, is to use all of your senses when visualizing. In this manner, you can trick the brain into believing that you are really in the place you are imaging. Scientists can now place people in functional magnetic resonance imaging scanners while they are imaging and see, for example, the engagement of the part of the brain that controls vision, the visual cortex.

In our experience, doing guided imagery can sometimes evoke powerful feelings in a student. For example, one student felt deep grief when she visualized a place where her deceased loved one had been. So, before you start the exercise, you should tell the students that they might have strong feelings, and that this is natural and nothing to worry about.

There are many research studies examining the effects of guided imagery on outcomes for patients. You may choose to mention one of them, depending on the amount of available time. Information about this research can be found in chapter 4.

Music adds to the serenity in the room during guided imagery. We like the flute music of R. Carlos Nakai. For the imagery, we use a script (entitled "Safe Place") developed at the Center for Mind–Body Medicine in Washington, D.C. With their permission, we have printed it here. Remember to read slowly, with pauses interspersed.

Allow yourself to sit back and relax . . .see that your arms and legs are in a position that feels right for you. And . . . .slowly and gently close your eyes.

[pause for about 10–15 seconds]

Allow your attention to move to your breathing. Let your breathing become even and comfortable. Breathing is one of the most powerful conscious influences you have on your nervous system.

[pause]

So now I'd like you to see yourself in a very special place . . . it could be a real place—a place you may actually have been—a beautiful spot in nature or a comforting place in your own home. Your special place may be an imaginary place—a place in fairy tales—indoors or outdoors—it doesn't really matter. Should more than one place come to mind, allow yourself to stay with one of them. . . .

[pause]

The only thing that matters is that it is a place in which you are completely comfortable and safe. . . . You feel comfortable and safe. . . . Appreciate this scene with all of your senses. . . . Hear the sounds—smell the aromas, feel the air as it caresses your skin—experience the ground securely under you—touch and feel the whole environment that you are in.

[pause]

Notice what you are wearing.

[Short pause after this instruction and each one that follows]

Notice what you have on your feet.
What time of year is it? What time of day?
How old are you?
Are you alone or with another person or people?
Notice the colors that surround you.
What is the temperature? Is it warm? Is it cold?
Notice the qualities of the place that make it safe and comfortable.

[pause]

And look around you to see if there is anything else that would make this place more
safe for you. . . . Perhaps something that you need to remove from the place or
something you need to bring in. . . . And then notice how your body feels in this place
. . . and now take some time to enjoy this feeling of safety in your special place. . . .
(allow several minutes before moving on.)

[pause]

And now thank yourself for taking the time. . . this time for yourself and perhaps
promising yourself . . . and reassuring yourself . . . that you will visit this place or
some other place on your own whenever you need to.

[pause]

And when you are ready . . . at your own pace . . . let your breathing deepen. . . . Very
gradually let the awareness of your body against the chair return. . . . Bring yourself
back slowly and comfortably. . . . And now when you are ready . . . and only when
you are ready . . . gently open your eyes with a smile on your face.

The students' responses to guided imagery have been overwhelmingly positive. In the evaluations, there are often requests for more time with this skill.

This is what the students say about this skill:

"I particularly loved the guided imagery exercise. I've already felt some of the benefits of these techniques and expect they will be even more rewarding as I grow and progress with them. Thank you, guys!"

"A whole class on guided imagery would be awesome!"
"Guided imagery revealed interesting things about myself."

Guided Meditation: Labeling Thoughts

The guided meditation during the third class is designed to give the students more help in working with their thoughts, as this is often the greatest obstacle for them. "Labeling" thoughts is a useful technique for managing a busy mind, so that is the focus of the guided meditation in the third class. You will teach the students to practice labeling their thoughts and letting them go, coming back to their breath as often as they can. The following is an example of how this meditation might be introduced:

Today we're going to spend some time improving our ability to work with the thoughts that are always being created by our minds. Thoughts pull our attention away from our awareness of the fullness of our present-moment experiences, into the world of worries, judgments, memories, and plans. We'll work a little with using labels to help you notice and release your thoughts as they arise. When you label or name a thought, it helps you bring the thought more into the awareness of observing mind, and it becomes easier to watch the thought without getting carried away by it. The simplest way to use labels is to say silently to yourself "thinking" every time you become aware that you are thinking, then return your attention gently to your breath.

If you notice that your thoughts are all focused on a theme like judging or planning, it can be useful to apply the labels "judging" or "planning" to those thoughts. Other labels, like "remembering" or "wanting," can also be useful. It's not helpful to spend a lot of time trying to decide what label to use. If you notice that you are doing this, just label it all "thinking" and keep returning to the breath. Remember, we're not trying to stop our thinking; we're just trying to get better at noticing it. This meditation is really about practicing our ability to notice our thoughts and come back to the present moment over and over again.

A sample script for the meditation follows:

(Ring the bell before starting and remember to progress slowly through the meditation, giving the students time to work with each instruction. Try to spend 15–20 minutes on this meditation, pausing for a few seconds between each sentence of the instruction and using longer pauses of a minute or more between the paragraphs.)

Let's get back into our meditation position: feet on the floor, hands resting in our laps, backs straight, eyes closed. Let's begin by taking a moment to notice the feeling of your feet resting against the floor. Notice the feeling of your hands in your lap. Notice the feeling of your body relaxing into the chair. . . .

[pause]

Now, when you feel ready, allow your attention to gently settle on your breath as you again find that place in your body where you can most easily feel the sensations of your breath moving in and out. . . .

[pause]

Watching, with curiosity, an entire in-breath . . .

[pause]

Watching, with a sense of warmth and patience, an entire out-breath . . .

[pause]

When you notice that your mind has wandered, see if you can briefly observe the thoughts, without judging them, perhaps label them "thinking," and then gently let them go, returning your awareness to the sensations of your breath, your anchor to your present-moment experience. . . .

[pause]

Again, when your mind has wandered, practice noticing that thoughts are arising. Try attaching a very gentle label to the thoughts as they arise, silently noting to yourself "thinking" . . ."judging," or . . . "planning," then gently let them go, returning your attention to your breath. . . .

[pause]

If you're lost in thought, notice that, label it, and gently return your attention to the sensations of your breath, noting the rise and fall of your breath as it moves in and out of your body. Again, let your breath be your anchor to your present-moment experience. . . .

[pause; if you have time, allow 2–3 minutes of silence before proceding]

Where are your thoughts now?. . . . Can you notice and accept each thought? Letting it pass through your mind without clinging to it or judging it?. . .

(Allow several minutes before moving on.)

When you hear the bell ring, make a commitment to bring this level of awareness to all of your experiences today. (After the bell rings, invite the students to stretch.)

Closing Comments

After the guided meditation, you will pass out the logs for the next week. Briefly review the skills and meditations that have been introduced thus far (dynamic breathing, belly breathing, body scan, walking mediation, guided imagery, gatha, labeling thoughts) and remind the students that they can practice any of them for their daily homework. You should also remind them that there is only one more class, and encourage them to be very diligent with their practice in the coming week. Also, remind them to continue working with a daily-life mindfulness activity. You may want to introduce the idea that next week you will be talking more about ways for them to continue their mindfulness practice after this course ends. As they begin to leave the room, encourage the students to maintain *their* mindfulness as they go down the stairs and on to their next activities.

Frequently Asked Questions

Q: Last night when I meditated, I felt this amazing warmth spreading through my body and I felt almost like I was floating. It was really awesome. What do you think that was?

A: *As you continue to practice your meditation, you will notice all sorts of strange experiences, some of them more pleasant than others. These experiences are neither good nor bad, and it is helpful to suspend judgment of them, just as we practice letting go of judgments in other areas. One danger with the really enjoyable or interesting experiences is that we can get very attached to these experiences and then spend all future meditations trying to re-create them. And of course, the harder you try to force a particular result in meditation, the less likely you are to achieve it. So, see if you can just be aware of whatever arises for you, be curious about it without grasping it, and continue with your practice.*

Q: I've got a question about the gratitude part of the log. This week it was hard for me because I was kind of down. I could think of things to be grateful about, but I didn't *feel* grateful, so I didn't fill in the log. I didn't think I should just fake it. What do you think about that?

A: *We would encourage you to go ahead and take note of the things that are pretty good in your life, even if in the moment you don't actually feel a sense of gratitude. The point of the exercise is to bring your awareness to some of the good things in your life, regardless of how much gratitude you feel at that particular time. It's okay if it's just a cognitive exercise without a lot of emotional impact. Sometimes you may notice nice, warm, fuzzy feelings of thankfulness. At other times, you may feel grumpy and unhappy despite identifying several things in your life that you could feel grateful for. As with all of our mindfulness practices, we're not trying to force any particular feeling. We just want you to bring awareness to some of the positive aspects of your life. Be willing to observe and accept whatever response arises.*

Q: I really liked using the gatha this week. I found I was much better able to concentrate when I repeated the gatha when I meditated. Is it okay for me to use the gatha over and over or should I be trying to do something else?

A: *During this class you will learn many different calming skills and meditation techniques. We do not expect you to become expert in each of them. What we find is that different students respond to different skills and practices. One student may really love the gatha and find that's what helps him stay present the best; the next student may hate the gatha and feel most steadied by the belly breathing. If you find something that seems to work well for you, by all means use it and see how far it will take you. At the same time, we want to encourage you to remain curious about and open to the skills that are still to come. You may be surprised to find yourself resonating with several of the techniques you learn. Also, you will likely notice that the skill that is most helpful when you are tired—say, dynamic breathing—is not the skill that is most helpful when you are restless or irritable. That's another reason that it can be useful to become familiar and comfortable with more than one approach to developing mindfulness.*

One last thing. I notice that you say "Is it okay?" I just want to remind you that we're also practicing letting go of judgment and the habit of dividing our experiences into "okay" and "not-okay" groups. As you continue to practice, see if you can notice the times that your mind wants to decide if you are "right" or not. Practice observing the pull to judge, and see what happens if you just let the situation be as it is. For example, you are noticing that your mind focuses better when you use the gatha. That's a very useful observation. Stay curious about whether that continues to be true for you or if, over time, other practices seem to become more effective for you personally. There is no right or wrong way of being mindful. The second you start paying attention to what your body or mind is doing, you are wonderfully and perfectly mindful!

Q: Well, I didn't like the gatha that much. I found all the words annoying. I've been using the walking meditation and trying to do belly breathing at night. I find it helps me go to sleep most of the time, but sometimes I seem to get more nervous when I try to start controlling my breath.

A: Perfect! It's so nice to have a demonstration, right in front of us, of the way different people resonate with different practices. One student loves the gatha and finds it useful; the next student finds it too distracting. If we can remember that we all have different perspectives, we can begin to let go of our judgments.

Now, back to your issue. What you are describing, getting more nervous when you begin to focus on your breath, is not uncommon. I find it relates to a sense of trying to control the breath rather than just observing it, allowing yourself to be curious about it without needing it to be different. Letting go of control in general can be quite hard. We all spend much of our waking time trying to plan and control everything about our lives. It's not surprising that when we turn our attention to our breath, we start to feel that we need to regulate it as well. The truth is, your body will (and does all the time) keep on breathing without any conscious assistance at all from your planning mind. Like everything else about learning these skills, it takes practice to learn to observe your breath without trying to interfere with it. One trick to try is to imagine your breath as rolling waves on an expansive ocean. Watch the rise and fall of the ocean swells, seeing how they have their own natural rhythm. Relax into the moment, letting your breath rise and fall along with the waves. Accept your breath as it is in this moment. Let it be.

Do this for just a few minutes at a time at first. If you start noticing anxiety or tension arising, then move your focus to other sensations in your body the way we do in the body scan: feeling the sensations in your feet and hands, noticing the way your body feels resting in the chair or on the bed.

Most importantly, don't give up. Those of us who have trouble letting go of control and have a tendency to get nervous at times are the ones who stand to gain the most from learning these skills. It is natural to find them to be challenging and not immediately helpful until you have practiced more with them. Allow yourself to remain open-minded, reserving judgment and continuing to do your 10 minutes of daily practice. Be willing to just see what happens.

Q: I was feeling stressed and having a hard time getting my work done this week. I remembered what you were saying about just paying attention to the feeling of my fingers tapping on the keyboard. It worked better than I thought it would. Every time I'd start worrying, I'd remind myself just to pay attention to what I was actually doing. I think it helped me get my work done faster.

A: Great! I'm glad you were able to give that a try. If you continue to pay attention, you will likely notice that there are all sorts of situations in which you are lost in judging or worrying thoughts. Once you notice the thoughts, you can decide to let them go by turning your attention to your present-moment experience. I can't tell you how many times I've been in perfectly lovely situations, like walking through Duke Gardens on a gorgeous day, and I became aware that my thoughts were off somewhere else, fretting about something and making me feel stressed. But once I became aware and then started to pay attention to my beautiful surroundings, I immediately felt more relaxed.

Q: I'm still having a lot of trouble practicing regularly. I've been really bad this week. Procrastination is a huge problem with everything I do, including this meditation stuff. I'm feeling really frustrated.

A: Have you been REALLY BAD? REALLY, REALLY BAD? What would it look like if you were really good? Maybe if you meditated an hour every day? How about an hour twice a day? Then you'd be REALLY GOOD! Is there any gray space in between? I find that the standards we hold ourselves to for being good are usually absurdly high. For example, I think that signing up for this class and coming to the sessions is really, really good. Most people wouldn't even move that far in the direction of personal growth and greater awareness. A less judgmental way of thinking about this is to notice that it felt hard to get started with meditation and be curious about what strategies you can employ to get through it.

Which brings us to procrastination, which is a huge issue for many students. Has anyone else in the room ever had trouble with procrastination? Gee, what a surprise, all hands are raised! So, you are not alone.

Procrastination often arises because the thought of getting started on our task is too unpleasant and aversive, maybe because the task seems too hard or doesn't seem very interesting or maybe just because we don't know where to start. Often the thoughts that go along with this have to do with how long it will take to finish or how hard it will be to do the task perfectly. What are the thoughts you have when you notice you are procrastinating about starting meditation? Are they similar to the thoughts you have when you are procrastinating about some other task?

Q: Usually I'm thinking that I'll start meditating as soon as I do something else. Or I'm thinking that I don't know what I'm doing or just that I don't want to do it. I just dread getting started.

A: "Dread" is a good word to describe the feeling many people have when they are trying to start doing something that is aversive for them. Can you just sit with the feeling, try not to judge it, and then shift your attention to the sensations in your body as you move ahead with your task?

For example, if you remember that you need to do your meditation practice but just don't feel like getting started, notice the feeling of "not wanting to" and then move your attention to your body as you sit or stand in that moment. If you are standing, take a seat and notice how that feels in your body. Notice any thoughts you have about not wanting to meditate or not knowing how to do it or liking it or not liking it. Anything at all can come up. As soon as you start becoming aware of these physical sensations and your thoughts and feelings, you ARE MEDITATING. You've already started. Perhaps then you can carry on for a few minutes and see what happens.

Q: But I hate that feeling of dread I get when I have a big paper to write or a test to study for. I want it to be easier!

A: *Of course you do. We all want our bad feelings to be gone and life to be easier. Once again, we find that you are perfectly normal! The truth is, though, that sometimes we have uncomfortable feelings. The more we fight and struggle against them, the worse things get for us. It's okay to feel dread about getting started writing. It's okay to not like the feeling of dread. It may help to understand that the task is not to make the dread go away; the task is to recognize that the bad feeling is impermanent and you can get on with things in spite of it. This is where acceptance and present-moment awareness come in and can be really useful.*

   When you start to pay attention to your present-moment experience, you'll see that the feeling of dread will go away, and it will come back sometimes and it will go away again. That's what feelings do. They come and they go. This is true of wonderful, joyful feelings as well as uncomfortable feelings. Because we are wonderfully human and our lives are complex, our feelings are coming and going and shifting all the time. We have difficulty when we believe that our behaviors must always be determined by our feelings. In reality, we feel what we feel. These feelings certainly influence our behavior, but they don't have to determine it completely.

   In this example, the feeling of dread has nothing to do with whether you complete the task at hand. You can start writing your paper in spite of the bad feeling. If you notice that you feel dread, just feel dread. I'm not saying it's easy, but then you've done a lot of things in your life that weren't easy. We don't just wait around for things to get easy, do we? Notice the uncomfortable emotion, then turn your attention to the physical sensations as you sit in front of your computer or open your book and begin working. Notice the feeling of your fingers on the keyboard or the feeling of the pages of your book in your hand. Keep your awareness in just that moment. When you notice thoughts such as "I hate this . . . I'll never get done . . . I don't want to do this," just observe them and bring your attention back to the work. They are just thoughts. You can even label them "dreading," which may help you let them go. Labeling is a skill we're going to practice later today. Focus fully on the words you are reading or the concepts you are working with, letting go of the distracting thoughts about how the work is going or how you feel about the work. Although you don't need the bad feeling to go away before you start working, it is likely that it will go away when you are focused on the moment-to-moment experience of writing a paper or solving math problems. The paradox of mindfulness is at work again; when you no longer fight against your dread and get on with your business, the feeling of dread goes away on its own.

Q: I'm having a similar problem, trouble practicing regularly, but for me it's still mainly to do with time. I've tried different times and places, but I just can't get anything to work. I still feel as though I just don't have time to do it.

A: Time is a funny thing, isn't it? It can be so subjective. We've all experienced the way time seems to drag when we're waiting for something to happen or the way it flies by when we're having a good time. Maybe your sense that you don't have enough time is due in part to the way you think about your time. For example, do you ever spend time waiting, such as waiting in line at the store or waiting for someone to meet you? How do you feel when you're waiting? Impatient? Stressed? What if you decide to use your waiting time as your mindfulness time? What if, every time you found yourself waiting, you brought your attention to your breath and watched the in-and-out of your breathing? Do you think that would change the way it feels to wait and the way you experience that "wasted" time? Perhaps there are other places in your day when you have "wasted" time that could have been used for practicing mindfulness. Try this week to pay close attention to how you spend your time and think about your time, and see if you don't notice some spaces opening up for practicing mindfulness.

Q: For some reason, this week things really started to click for me with the meditation. I'm starting to feel less anxious. I'm getting better at noticing when I'm worrying and bringing my mind back to the present. Sometimes, though, the worry is so strong that I just can't let go of it. What should I do then?

A: Worry, especially intense, anxious worry, is one of the hardest thought patterns to release. Anxious worries just dig in and don't let go; you'll notice the way your thoughts can go round and round. Intense worry is probably one of those 200-pound weights we talked about before—the kind of powerful emotional and cognitive experience that takes a lot of mindfulness practice to be able to work with.

    If you notice what is going on when you are worrying, you will probably see that worry is very future-oriented. When we are worried, we are thinking about what might happen. There are lots of "what if" and "what then" kinds of thoughts. We can come up with all sorts of catastrophes that might happen. Our mind dwells on worst-case scenarios, resulting in intense anxiety along with physical discomfort. We can feel muscle tension, stomach aches, even chest pain and heart palpitations.

You may be surprised to hear that worry is not possible if you maintain present-moment awareness. Really. I'll say it again. Worry is not possible if you maintain present-moment awareness. What sorts of things do you find you worry about?

Q: Well, different things. Sometimes it is about school stuff. But lately I've been worrying about stuff with my girlfriend, like she's going to lose interest or break up or something.

A: *That's a typical example of the sorts of things we worry about. In this case your mind moves into the future, wrestling with something that you fear could happen but is in fact not happening right now. You start thinking about "What if that happens?" and "What will I do?" and "How will I cope?" and on and on. This is all future-oriented thinking.*

The first thing to do is to try to get your thoughts back into the present. To do this when you are really worrying, you will probably need to practice one of the more active skills. Dynamic breathing is a great one to try if you are feeling really worried. You can do dynamic breathing for a few minutes, then try to shift to a movement meditation like walking meditation. Belly breathing can be very helpful here because it is so calming. Physical sensations are probably the most potent anchors for your attention, so going outside to feel the wind and sun can help.

If you are able to move your mind into the present, you might notice intense emotions coming up: sadness, fear, guilt, anger. You might notice muscle tension or other physical sensations. You might notice wanting things to be different or resolved. Some of this will likely be very uncomfortable, but if you can stay with it and just observe what is going on without judging it, you are less likely to end up paralyzed by anxiety. After a while, if you can stay with present-moment awareness, you'll likely notice that the feelings start to shift, and the intensity may decrease. You may find that you can begin to think clearly about what you need to do to address the issues in your relationship and feel calm enough to talk effectively with your girlfriend about these things.

Again, I really respect the fact that this is a 200-pound weight—maybe a 500-pound weight. I'm not trying to say that meditating in this situation is simple or easily learned. But it is possible. It is possible to learn to face your most difficult moments in a completely different way, to take an approach that cultivates wisdom and good decisions, patience and compassion. Like everything else worth doing, it takes practice. With practice, you can begin to see that in this moment, you are okay. You may feel some intense emotional discomfort, but if you are fully present, you will also be able to notice that you are slowly breathing in and out, the sun is warm on your face, and the sky is a very deep blue. Pay attention. Stay present. Don't judge it. Let it pass.

The Fourth Class

The fourth class is the final class in the course. The students have been practicing for 3 to 4 weeks and thus have a significant amount of experience with the theory and practice of mindfulness. In addition to teaching a new skill and practicing more meditation, one of the primary tasks of this class is to introduce the students to options for continuing their new practice. The comments, both spoken and written, that students tend to make during this class demonstrate that most of them have experienced some form of transformation. They are excited about the progress they have made, and many are motivated to continue. Supporting their sense of optimism about the potential for change inherent in their new practice can be balanced by telling them that they will have to work hard if they want to deepen the learning they have begun. Helping them find a direction for further learning and practice is critical.

Overview

Begin by collecting and commenting on the logs as the students are gathering for the class. Much like the second class, in the fourth class the students often have a lot to say, so check-in can be quite lengthy. They may feel that this is the last chance they will have to ask questions about their new practice and share their experience with the group. You should also invite them to share any general feedback about the course verbally during check-in.

Mindful Eating

The mindfulness skill you will teach in the fourth and final class is mindful eating. Mindful eating is a skill that students can use to enhance their pleasure in eating, as well as their ability to return their minds to the present moment. Because the act of eating is something we generally take for granted, it can be quite enlightening for the students to observe all the flavors and textures they are missing when they spend their meals watching an electronic screen of some sort. This skill seems to be the best one to save for last, as we are

---

CHAPTER 9: KEY POINTS

- In the fourth and final class, it is important to leave room for both verbal and written feedback from the students.
- Eating meditation, the skill taught in this class, develops mindfulness, increases the pleasure of eating, and has important physiological effects.
- Labeling feelings during meditation helps the students notice their feelings without getting overwhelmed by them.
- The students will need information about resources for continuing their training in mindfulness. You should stress that they will need to seek further training and support if they wish to continue to deepen their practice.

---

mainly introducing the students to the idea of mindful eating and they are less likely to have technical questions about the skill after they've practiced it on their own.

The guided meditation in the fourth class is focused on mindfulness of feelings. This meditation builds on the practice the students have had with using labels to help them stay mindful of their thoughts. You will introduce the idea of using labels when feelings arise to help the students stay present with their feelings without becoming overwhelmed by them.

Finally, leave time at the end of the class for the students to complete a written evaluation of the course. Students' feedback has proved invaluable to us as we adapted our course to better meet the needs of our learners.

Opening Meditation

As in the other classes, this meditation should last for about 5 minutes. Pause between each instruction for 15–20 seconds.

It is so good to see everyone here today. Why don't you stretch a little and then get into your meditation positions. . . .

[pause]

Close your eyes. . . .

[pause]

If you are feeling sleepy, remember that you can keep your eyes open and gaze at the floor to help you stay awake. . . .

[pause]

Now, let's see if we can bring ourselves into this moment by focusing on our breath. You might need to use counting or the gatha to help your focus. . . .

[pause]

Just let yourselves sink into the present moment, noticing thoughts when they arise without judging. . . .

[pause]

Giving yourself the gift of being fully present with this moment. . . .

[pause]

Nothing else is happening, just this moment. . . .

[pause]

When you hear the bell, see if you can bring your attention to the sound until it has completely faded away.

[Ring the bell, then pause until the sound has faded]

And stretch!

[Stretch your arms high over your head]

Check-in

You should begin check-in by observing that this is your last class together. You may want to comment on how well the students have progressed and how much you, the teachers, have enjoyed the class. As usual, you will go around the circle, inviting each student to share his or her experience of meditation practice over the previous week. Additionally, invite the students to share any comments or observations about the course in general. As in the preceding weeks, you will use their comments and questions as opportunities to teach them more about mindfulness. See the "Frequently Asked Questions" section at the end of the chapter for typical questions and our responses.

Once the check-in is complete, you can take a few moments to summarize what you have just heard from the students. You should then stress that if they want to continue their mindfulness practice, you strongly recommend that they make plans to attend a meditation group or class. In our experience, students who wish to continue practicing will need additional support. You can tell them that they will receive at the end of class a "Next Steps Guide" (see appendix E) that has lists of books, Web sites, classes, groups, and retreat centers that they can access to continue their training in mindfulness.

Although we want the students to continue their training, we recognize that what they've learned in the mindfulness and meditation course will continue to benefit them, whether they get more training or not. By the time students finish the course, they have gained a new understanding of what causes stress and ways to manage their experience of stress. They have learned the value of bringing their attention to the present moment, and most of them have achieved insight and growth as a result. This understanding will persist, even if they don't seek further training in mindfulness.

Here are some typical student comments during check-in of the final class:

"I really like guided imagery. I love going to the beach! I wish we had done more of it in class."

"I noticed this week that if I do my 10 minutes in the morning, my whole day is better."

"My mindfulness activity that we're supposed to do every day was really hard to do. I tried to be mindful when I was brushing my teeth but, man, there was no way!"

"I'm really sad that the class is over. Four weeks is just too short a time."

Skills Training: Eating Meditation

You will need grapes or raisins for introducing eating meditation to the students. It's a good idea to keep the food hidden so that the students can't see it before the exercise begins.

We introduce this mindfulness practice by asking the students if they have ever eaten a meal without doing something else at the same time. The students always laugh as they realize that they always eat while sitting in front of the computer or talking with friends or watching TV or reading or texting. We, the teachers, relate to this situation. We know that eating mindfully opens a new world for our students, as it has for us. You may want to tell your own stories of discovering that you automatically do other things while eating—for example, eating lunch in your office while working at the computer. Ask the students to imagine how much pleasure in eating has passed them by while they had their attention on something else. They realize immediately that this is true, that they often don't fully enjoy good food. You can then invite them to be curious about this new practice.

Take a moment to mention another benefit of mindful eating: that slowing down helps your brain know when you are full, at the right time, so that you are unlikely to eat too much. In addition, paying more attention to your food might help you to make healthier food choices.

When you are ready to start the exercise, give the following instructions slowly, allowing the students time to fully experience all the evoked sensations. Pause between each instruction to allow the students to fully experience each step of the meditation. (This script is used with grapes. You will need to adapt it slightly if you are using raisins or other food.)

Please get into your meditation position with your eyes closed. Let your hands rest quietly in your lap, one hand on top of the other, palms up. I am going to place an object in your hand, and I want you to let it rest there without any movement. . . .

[pause]

Now, bring your awareness to the object. What does it feel like? What is the texture, the temperature, the weight? Do you notice your mind wondering what it might be or thinking that you know what it is?

[pause]

Now, open your eyes and bring your full attention to the object resting in your hand. Notice the color. Notice if the light shines on it differently in different places. Notice if there are smooth or rough places. Pretend that you have just landed on this planet and you have never seen an object like this. Notice any thoughts you are having as you look at the object. Are there any sensations in your mouth that might be signaling a wish to eat the object? Are you wondering what the point of this is? Are you waiting for this exercise to be over? Just notice the thoughts and bring your attention back to the object.

[pause]

Now, I'm about to tell you to bring the object up under your nose. Remember to concentrate on every movement it takes to move your hand and arm. Okay, go ahead. Just hold the object under your nose and notice the smell, what is happening in your mouth, your thoughts. . . . Then slowly open your mouth and place the object in it without chewing or swallowing it. Just let it rest in your mouth and notice everything that is happening in your mouth. Do you notice a desire to chew? Do you notice impatience? Do you notice salivation?

[pause]

Now, begin to chew very slowly and mindfully, noticing the taste, your tongue movements, texture, changes in texture and taste. Do not swallow yet. . . .

[pause]

Finally, you may begin to swallow. See if you feel the bits of food as they go down your esophagus.

When we ask the class if anyone wants to say anything about their experience of eating a grape (or raisin) in this manner, we often hear their amazement at how much flavor is in a single grape. Chances are that none of them has ever had this kind of experience with food. We don't expect them to be able to eat all of their meals mindfully, but we do encourage them to try a couple of easy practices: eating just one bite of a meal mindfully and/or putting the fork down between bites of food, as this slows everything down.

Guided Meditation: Labeling Feelings

The meditation in this class is designed to give the students more practice using labels, and to expand the practice to the awareness and labeling of feelings. It's the last guided meditation for the course and an important one, so try to make sure that you leave 15 minutes for it. Introduce the meditation by saying something like this:

> Just as we learned last week to use the label "thinking" when we notice our thoughts, we can also use the label "feeling" if we notice strong feelings arising. The process of labeling a feeling gives us a little distance from the sensation. It helps remind us that we are not our feelings. Rather, they are just phenomena that arise, change, and end, like everything else in the world. For example, you might notice feeling very nervous or anxious while you are meditating. This feeling is usually accompanied by a lot of repetitive worry thoughts. You can use the labels "worrying" and "anxious" to help strengthen your observing mind, allowing yourself to "sit on the bank" while those thoughts and feelings flow by. Maybe this practice will help you to feel curious about the feeling and how it changes, rather than fighting it and trying to force it to go away. Perhaps you can gain enough distance from it to relax into your present-moment experience, allowing the feeling to just be rather than struggling to change it or end it.

You can begin the guided meditation in the following manner, pausing between each instruction to give the students time to practice:

> *Let's begin by getting into our meditation position once more, feet flat on the floor, backs straight, hands resting in your lap. Allow your eyes to close and listen for the sound of the bell. . . .*

[Ring the bell, then pause]

Notice the feeling of your body resting in the chair, your hands resting in your lap, your feet resting on the floor. . . .

[pause]

Move your attention to the sensation of your breath, and let your awareness settle on that place in your body where you most easily feel your breath. . . .

[pause]

As you watch your breath, you will notice your mind moving and thoughts beginning to arise. As we learned last week, practice gently, silently labeling the thoughts and then releasing them. Thinking. Judging. Planning. Wanting. Noting whatever is there without judgment, then returning to the sensation of your breath. . . .

[pause]

You may notice that there are feelings or emotions, sometimes underneath the thoughts, sometimes without associated thoughts. Can you notice and label those feelings the same way you label thoughts? Calm, restless, sad, happy, angry, worried, excited, bored. . . . Gently label the feeling, then come back to the sensation of your breath, again using the breath as your anchor to your present-moment experience. . . .

[pause]

Notice. Are thoughts arising? Are feelings present? Label and come back to your breath. . . .

[pause]

(If there is time, give the students several minutes of silence to practice labeling their feelings before moving on to the next instruction.)

Where is your mind now?

[pause]

When you hear the bell ring, make a commitment to bring this same level of awareness to all of your activities.

Class Evaluation, "Next Steps Guide," and Closing Remarks

Plan to leave 5 or 10 minutes at the end of the class for students to complete the written evaluation (appendix F); the evaluations are anonymous, so the students leave them face down in the center of the room when they are finished. Before they leave, give them each a copy of your resource guide (our example, the "Next Steps Guide," is presented in appendix E) and extra logs to use if they wish to continue to chart their practice for the next 2 weeks.

Stress again the importance of trying another class or group, and if you are comfortable with this, invite the students to contact you at any time in the future if they have questions or want guidance about continuing their meditation practice. Thank the students for their commitment to the course, and remind them once again to carry their mindfulness with them as they walk down the stairs and move into the beautiful day.

Once the students are gone, spend a few minutes reviewing the evaluations and thinking about what you have learned from this particular group. We anticipate that you will share our experience of feeling impressed by the depth of their learning and touched by the gratitude they express for their new skills. We notice our own gratitude as we recognize that these students transform us as they are transformed by mindfulness.

Frequently Asked Questions

Q: The eating meditation was really interesting. I've never enjoyed a grape so much in my life! But I don't understand how I'd eat a meal mindfully. It would take forever.

A: *Eating an entire meal mindfully does indeed take a long time, but it is a great meditation practice and worth trying. Having a mindful cup of tea can be a powerful mindfulness exercise to bring you into the present, letting go of worries and doubts. In general, though, eating mindfully doesn't have to involve an entire meal; even small amounts of mindful eating can be beneficial. Try eating just the first bite of every meal mindfully. It's a great way to start a meal and will generally set you up to be more aware of the rest of the meal, even if you aren't doing a very slow meditative eating of the whole meal. Anything that slows your eating down a little can add to your mindfulness; we suggest putting your fork down between each bite and noticing what happens. You are likely to find that you pay more attention and get more satisfaction from your meal just by making this one change. Of course, just making an effort to turn off the computer or TV while eating will help you slow down, pay more attention to your food, and give you a better idea of when you are full.*

Q: I've been trying to label my thoughts. Can you say more about how that works? I sometimes find it helpful, but at other times I find that I'm just thinking about labels!

A: *Remember the metaphor about the river? We talked about our mind being a racing river, with a torrent of thoughts traveling along it almost constantly. Mindfulness is the skill that allows us to sit on the bank, at peace, watching the river rush by. Without mindfulness, we are in the river being washed away. Labeling thoughts works like a rope that you can use to pull yourself back onto the bank. Each time we label a thought, we gain a little distance from it, a little perspective; observing mind makes a little headway with thinking mind This slight change in your relationship to your thinking allows you to drop into the present moment. Right now, I'm thinking. Right now, I'm planning. Right now, I'm wanting. Can you say more about your experience in working with labels?*

Q: Well, I did find that I could bring myself back using labels. But sometimes I'd just be completely checked out for a long time before I noticed. Once I noticed, I'd want to label, but then I'd begin thinking about what I'd been thinking about! Like I was trying to figure out what to label and ended up just spending more time thinking.

A: *You do have to watch out for the trap of thinking too much about the labels. That's why the generic term "thinking" can be so useful. I've discovered that the vast majority of my thoughts can be labeled planning: planning what I'll say to whom or when I'll do what. It's quite funny, really. Sometimes I can even catch myself planning what label to use. Then I really laugh at myself. Anytime I find myself in those kinds of circular thought patterns, I just go back to using thinking because it helps me get back into observing mind. If you begin to notice a pattern of always wanting to find the perfect label, you might find that there are other times when your thoughts are about wanting things to be just right or a certain way. It can be very interesting to notice the pattern of "wanting" and to use that as your label. But the main thing is to not get too caught up in picking a label or you'll find that you've been washed away by the river yet again. And remember, the moment you notice that you are checked out, you are no longer checked out; you are back in the present.*

Let me say a little more about what we call "wanting mind." One of the ways we create suffering for ourselves is by spending a lot of time wanting things, people, feelings, experience, and so on that we don't have. Noticing this mindset is an important insight that evolves with mindfulness training. It is really helpful to notice that you want things to be different than they are right now. Wanting, or grasping as it is sometimes called, is the opposite of acceptance. How much time do you spend wanting things to be different? Honestly, we all want things to be different much of the time, don't we? And when something feels good, we want it to last longer, right? So, wanting mind is a very big part of us. And, as always with mindfulness, when we can notice wanting, we have a chance of not allowing ourselves to be caught up in it. Wanting mind causes a lot of unpleasant feelings, including anxiety, stress, sadness, and anger. "I don't like this. I wish it weren't happening. Why is it happening? If only things were different, then I'd be happy." Once you notice all of this struggle against the way things are in the moment, you can make a thoughtful decision about whether you can change anything or not. And then you're right back at acceptance.

Q: I feel like I've made a lot of progress. I'm feeling less stressed, and that's cool. But I'm still having a hard time with acceptance. I mean, I don't know how to decide to accept things.

A: You may be getting hung up on the idea that you have to "decide" about acceptance. Acceptance is not a cognitive exercise. It's not about thinking and deciding to accept something. Acceptance is simply becoming aware, because when you become aware, you see things as they are. In that moment, you let go of the need for anything to be different because you are just seeing things as they are. No judgment. No struggle. So, if you are in a situation you don't like, you don't have to decide to accept it. You certainly don't have to decide to like it. All you have to do is become aware of how you are feeling and thinking in this moment. As soon as you bring your awareness to your present-moment experience, you are experiencing acceptance. Deciding to accept a situation is just more thinking; noticing how this moment feels is the act of acceptance.

Q: I can't believe how much this class has changed me. I don't want to lose all the progress I've made. What should I do to keep this going?

A: It's so nice to hear your motivation to continue learning. As wonderful as our accomplishment together has been, you have just seen the beginning of the changes that mindfulness can bring to your life. If you continue to practice and learn, you will be amazed at how profoundly this new way of being can alter your life. I sometimes think back to the way I used to be, the way I thought about the world, say, when I was a medical student. I can remember how I worried about my performance in school at the expense of just experiencing the learning opportunities. I remember the way I used to judge myself and everyone else. It's almost like remembering someone else's experience, because my mind doesn't work that way anymore. And it's not because I decided that I didn't want to think that way anymore. I didn't even realize that it might be helpful to think about things differently! The change occurred because I began studying and practicing mindfulness. Once you develop the habit of awareness, it changes the way you interact with all of your experience. It sounds like you have already begun to *experience some of this for yourself; stay curious about what may unfold if you continue to practice and just keep going!*

The best way to keep this going is to find a group to sit with every week or every other week. Or sign up for another class. Unfortunately, the dominant culture is not supportive of a mindful approach to life. We've got to make an effort to create space in our lives that is intentionally devoted to working on these concepts and skills. We'll be giving you all a list of resources for continuing your learning. We strongly encourage you to take the next step by joining another class or group.

Q: I just want to say that I feel like I'm thinking about things differently now. For example, last week was super busy for me. Usually when I have a week like that, I spend all this time thinking about everything I have to get finished, and worrying about it, and being stressed about it. But this time, I kept reminding myself to stay in the moment, you know, just do one thing at a time. If I caught myself worrying about everything I had to do later, I just remembered to let it go. I used dynamic breathing several times to do this. It felt good to see that I could change the way I was doing things.

A: Thanks for sharing that with us. Isn't it amazing to see how much of our stress is caused not by all the things we have to do, but instead by how we think about all the things we have to do? I continue to be amazed at the way my own stress level ratchets down if I stay focused on what needs to happen in this moment, right here, right now. The trick, of course, is to remember to catch yourself when you start cataloging everything you have to do all week. Again, it is in that moment of noticing, that moment of remembering, that we are once again anchored in the present.

One idea that I hope you are clear on now is the way that your thoughts about a situation, even more than the situation itself, create stress. You can be sitting under a beautiful tree on a sunny day and feel completely stressed out if your thoughts are about your fear that you won't make the grades you want at the end of the semester. This is very important. If you can bring your attention into the present moment, by becoming aware of your breath or other physical sensations, you can profoundly change your experience of stress. It's an awesome trick—simple but not easy. Yet, all of you have come a long way toward developing this skill, and that's something to be proud of. Try to stay curious about how far you can take it and keep practicing.

PART THREE

Conclusion

Transformation

- I have found that mindfulness has pervaded my life, on and off. I realize that my mind is spinning, and it has become much easier for me to take some breaths and bring my mind back to the present. I have found I'm worrying less because I have better control over my mind. Thank you!
- Meditation has surely become a part of my daily life, and mindfulness will change (and has changed) the way I do and see things.
- I wish this was a requirement for my nursing program!
- Without this class I might have flunked out of grad school in my first semester. What a gift!
- This class is the best thing (by far) I've done here at Duke. I can't wait to continue this practice and search out other groups and possibly retreats where I can learn and practice meditation.
- I wish there was a way to make these classes more accessible to medical students because we need it!

These six quotations are taken from written evaluations completed by our students anonymously at the end of the last Koru class.

When we started these courses in 2005, neither of us anticipated the depth of the transformation that many of our students would experience in just four classes. Initially, our goals for our students mirrored their goals for themselves: less worry and stress, greater happiness, improved academic performance, and improved sleep. Our hope was that we could, in some small way, help them move toward the improved quality of life they were seeking. To our great surprise and pleasure, the students have taught us that they are capable of much more, many of them expressing to us their sense of having been transformed in important ways. We believe that such transformation reflects the strengths of this age group: quickness, openness, willingness, eagerness. We have seen that the students who come to us are primed for change and eager to learn.

CHAPTER 10: KEY POINTS

- Meaningful transformation can occur for emerging adults who begin to practice mindfulness and meditation.
- Written evaluations are a key resource for assessing the students' transformation and for developing the course.
- Not all students will find every skill helpful. Teaching a broad range of skills allows each student to find something that is meaningful and effective for him or her.
- Through the evaluations, the students reveal how the course nourishes their positive beliefs about themselves:
  o I am not alone.
  o I am learning to accept myself.
  o I know myself better.
  o I can change. I am not stuck.
  o I can manage my relationships more thoughtfully.
  o I am not so overwhelmed or anxious. I have tools to help me deal with difficult feelings and difficult situations.

What is transformation, and what evidence do we have that these four simple classes facilitate transformation in emerging adults? Transformation entails a profound shift in a person's sense of identity and his or her place in the world. For example, one student described her transformation as follows:

> I notice the "negative energy" of my friends now. I hear them complaining about their boyfriends or work, and I don't feel drawn to it anymore. I feel like I can see that it's not where I want to put my energy anymore.

As we discussed in chapters 2 and 3, the developmental characteristics of emerging adults make them ripe for this type of change. We believe that the students' own evaluations of their experiences while learning mindfulness indicate that most of them have in fact gone through a significant transformation. In this chapter, we will look at our course evaluations, our most concrete source of student feedback, and what they show us about the students' perspectives on what they have achieved.

First, though, we will describe in more detail how we have used the evaluations and the information they contain. We will then look more specifically at our evaluation form and get a sense of how the students have responded by quoting them directly. Next, we will describe our own observations as we have witnessed the students transforming before our eyes. Finally, we will turn our attention to the growth and insights that the students feel have been most important for them.

The Students' Experiences: Written Evaluation

How do we know—and how will you know—that the model described in this book gives students a solid foundation for addressing the tasks and goals they articulate? How does mindfulness practice impact their ability to manage their stress, know themselves better, make thoughtful choices, and generally get greater fulfillment from life? In fine-tuning our model for teaching mindfulness and meditation, we have relied on feedback from the students to answer these questions. Our method of assessing the impact of the course has been to ask the students to provide detailed written evaluations at the end of the final class. We have measured the quality of the class by the students' reports of the benefits they have experienced and what in particular they have found helpful. We have made adjustments based on their comments and then tracked whether the changes were well-received by the next group of students. Although we have not used formalized screening instruments to quantify the improvements, we have found these descriptive data from the students useful for our purposes.

Over the last several years, we have received these descriptive data from nearly 200 students. Perhaps surprisingly, we have not received any overall negative evaluations; the students, for the most part, are tremendously gratified by the changes they are making. Students have judged specific aspects of the classes as more or less helpful, but all have reported that they experienced meaningful change.

Of course, there are some students who don't attend all the classes, despite our making attendance mandatory. We have noted different reasons for these absences. Some students miss a class simply because last-minute commitments kept them away temporarily. These students usually e-mail us to apologize and then return in later classes. Other students write to tell us that their schedules have changed and they simply cannot fulfill their commitment. Still others simply do not come to the first class or stop coming. This last group is fairly small; you may want to consider contacting such students to learn more about why they did not complete the course. These students may have found that they did not resonate with the teachings and therefore, had they stayed, might not have evaluated the class positively. However, this group is a minority of the participants; most students take the full course and complete the evaluation at the end.

In our model, the written evaluation serves several important functions, and we strongly recommend that you implement some sort of written feedback for your course. First, it helps you to get a general sense of how well you are communicating and connecting with the students. Second, it provides valuable information about which particular aspects of the course are working or not working for the students. Third, the process of completing the evaluation serves as a review and reminder for the students as they think about the class and articulate their responses. And fourth, the evaluations provide a written record of the responses to your classes. We have been gratified by how seriously the students take the evaluation, most spending time to thoughtfully complete the entire form.

If you decide to use this kind of evaluation, we advise you to hand the forms to the students after the final meditation in the last class. It is a good idea to ask the students to sit quietly while they complete the forms and then fold them and leave them on the floor in the center of the room so that they are anonymous. Our evaluations include the following questions:

1. What part of the class was most meaningful to you?
2. As a result of this class, what will you do differently in your life?
3. Was there anything you would have changed or added?
4. Please give feedback about:
   Check-in
   Logs
   Book
   Meditation practice at home
   CD
   Specific skills: belly breathing, dynamic breathing, walking meditation, eating meditation, guided imagery, use of the gatha and the body scan
5. Other feedback

The feedback we receive is almost 100% positive for questions 1, 2, 3, and 5—the general questions. We do not expect each part of the class to be a good fit for every student, though. Question 4 is where some students may report an aspect of the course that didn't work well for them. For example, sometimes a student will feel that **check-in** took up too much time during the class. We try to strike a balance between allowing room for the teaching and discussion that goes on during check-in, but we are aware that if we're not careful, it can take too much time. With practice, you will find that most of the time you are able to regulate this segment fairly well.

As for the **log**, most students say that they find it to be a good tool for reminding them to meditate. However, there are some students who do not find this kind of homework helpful. Here is a typical response from such a student: "I didn't enjoy the logs, made it feel like an assignment . . . but I did like the focus on gratitude." Almost all students gain inspiration from the **book**, but occasionally a student doesn't enjoy it: "I read it but didn't get much out of it. It was a little too much for me. Too far from how I think about and live life." A far more common answer is reflected in this student's words: "Very good book that puts your life into perspective and continuously emphasizes how a moment is essential because it is the piece of the puzzle that adds up to your whole life."

As to the **meditation practice at home,** many students express difficulty maintaining regular practice. "Change is difficult (still hard to fit in every day), but I am starting to see benefit in life." And finally, those students who use the **CD**—and not all do—find it helpful: "The CD is my favorite tool because I am still young in my meditation life."

The rest of question 4 addresses a wide variety of tools and skills. Many students say that they like learning the different skills: "Great to have such a variety to choose from. Really helpful to become familiar with and notice which would work best for me at which parts of the day and based on what is going on in my life at the time." Others praise specific skills:

- "Guided imagery revealed interesting things about myself."
- "I loved the surprise of feeling what simply smiling can do to my psyche."
- "Belly breathing, gatha, and the body scan help me fall asleep."

Occasionally, a student will report not liking the gatha. For example, one student commented, "The gatha we used sounded a little corny to me." This reflects a more general wariness of "new-agey" material that is fairly common among the students. You will need to watch for this skepticism and work with it when it arises. Noting it with respect and asking the students to remain open-minded and curious despite their skepticism seems to be an effective strategy for managing it.

Now, let's move to the general questions. Below are responses to questions 1, 2, and 3 that are selected to reflect the most common answers:

1. Most Meaningful

- The sense of community in the class, the sense of inner calm I had leaving class each week.
- Being able to be open with people about anxiety issues, knowing they won't judge because they are there for similar reasons.
- It was great to know that we're all in this together with similar concerns.
- The concept of observing mind (nonjudging). It really opened my eyes to accepting my thoughts rather than resenting them, learning about myself through meditation.

2. Will Do Differently

- I am already responding differently to stressful situations. I think I will continue to use the techniques I learned in these situations as well as in daily practice.
- I will make my decisions more mindfully with a fuller sense of self. I will try to take the time to enjoy the small wonders of life even in stressful situations and not forget/minimize the role of personal relationships, especially compared to career.
- I will surf the waves instead of running away from the ocean.
- I will make time to stop and breathe. And make good use of waiting.

3. Would Change or Add

- More classes!
- More classes!
- More classes!

(Yes, there is a common theme here! This answer has been by far the most frequent response to this question See chapter 5 for a discussion about the optimal number of classes in the Koru model)

Our Observations

In this small-group learning process with emerging adults, transformation comes quickly. Like us, you may find that it sometimes begins even before the course begins for those students who start reading the text in advance and are thereby introduced to mindfulness before the first class. The power of the group to transform is often evident in the first few minutes of the first class. We see the shift from students who are lost in their thoughts, on automatic pilot, to students who have already begun to be able to observe their thoughts and to feel hopeful about change. They are already beginning to see that mindfulness can help reduce their stress and anxiety. They hear each other's concerns at check-in and realize they are not alone, and this brings a measure of relief. They hear their classmates read their favorite quotations from the book, and the shift begins.

Sometimes this initial awareness brings discouragement as the students begin to notice their thoughts spinning out of control. They wonder how they will ever be able to stop all this thinking. And so, from the beginning, we emphasize over and over that this practice is *not* about stopping thinking and *not* about controlling thoughts. It is about *noticing*. This is one of the most profound aspects of mindfulness, and when your students start to understand it, you will see their relief. They come to believe that they have a chance to learn this thing called mindfulness.

Group cohesion increases quickly. It starts at the first check-in and grows steadily as the course progresses. Bonds form as students learn that they can trust you and each other. Hearts open and the students feel that they have the support they need for change. Only very rarely have we had a student who did not respond to the interpersonal warmth in the room.

As the course unfolds, there are noticeable changes in the students. We observe them developing their understanding as they ask increasingly complex questions. We see them improving their skills as the room gets progressively quieter when we sit in meditation. We hear the students report fundamental changes in their daily lives. They achieve greater self-acceptance as they practice nonjudging. They come to realize the values they hold most deeply. They notice how mindfulness positively affects their relationships. They believe that they can contemplate the future with less fear about the decisions and challenges facing them. They feel less overwhelmed. They feel that they have skills to help them when they are stressed, anxious, and exhausted. They have more confidence in their ability to make thoughtful decisions that spring from their true selves. All of these changes reflect common shifts in the students' underlying beliefs.

Beliefs and Insights

In reviewing the students' evaluations of their experience, we have seen certain responses and reactions expressed repeatedly. These common responses reflect underlying themes that are important to the students. They also show us the places where the students are developing new beliefs and insights.

I Am Not Alone

Our students tend to be hard on themselves, and they feel alone with many of their feelings and difficulties. Self-acceptance is a fruit of mindfulness practice, and for this age group, having the affirmation of their peers that they are not alone takes them a long way toward this acceptance. We see their relief during check-in as they indicate how they relate to each other's difficulties with practice and give each other suggestions. In fact, the most common answer on the written evaluation to question 1, about what was most meaningful, is that they no longer feel they are alone:

- "It was great to know that we're all in this together with similar concerns."
- "The weekly check-in to see where we are and to learn from others."
- "The check-in; it shows that you are not alone."
- "Hearing about others' experiences, questions, uncertainties, and enlightenments."
- "I think I learned and gained a lot from being part of the group and hearing about people's responses as well as giving mine."
- "The most meaningful was that this class provided a safe way to explore meditation. The combination of practice and discussion was a very nice structure."
- "Hearing everyone's experience during the hello and how they deal with different experiences not only helps me identify some ways [to help my practice] but reminds me that I also have some of those skills."

I Am Learning to Accept Myself

Developing acceptance and releasing judgment are important aspects of mindfulness that our emerging adults often find challenging. From the beginning, we advise you to emphasize the importance of developing these attitudes. The group dynamic that forms seems to facilitate this process. Feeling the support of a group of peers establishes a basis for learning. Students feel safe in the class and begin to see that some of their difficulties may be common in college life. This kind of insight is critical for their personal development as they begin the process of self-acceptance. They begin to understand that, ultimately, there is nothing wrong with them. And they can then begin to see how they judge themselves unnecessarily.

Many students have shared their insights about acceptance. Here are some reflections from students about what they felt was most meaningful in the course:

- "Most importantly to me: I am learning how to relax my "have to be a superwoman" complex and allowing myself to just be, even if that includes failure."
- "Hearing my classmates share their experiences from the week and then the feedback from Holly and Margaret. It was helpful to see the patterns emerge (i.e., the judgmental statements) and the reiteration that meditation isn't about making our thoughts stop."
- "Be more accepting of change and that I can judge without judging myself . . . yes!!"
- "[I will] be compassionate towards myself."

I Know Myself Better

How do our students get to know themselves better? Mindfulness practice itself enables them to pay more attention to what is happening and what they are thinking and feeling. They notice more clearly how they respond in challenging situations. They notice the feelings aroused and begin to name them. And as they learn mind–body skills and meditation, they learn which approaches "fit" them best in any given moment.

In addition, the gratitude portion of the logs helps deepen their awareness of who they are and what is going on in their lives and in themselves.

- "I have become a bit more able to gauge myself in situations, how my body feels and what I'm thinking/feeling."
- "[I will] stop trying to escape myself and instead awake to myself."
- "I am more aware of my body and state of mind. I am trying to prioritize the sense of calm that I enjoy now that I realize I can get there—so more time alone and unscheduled, less trips to the mall."

I Can Change; I Am Not Stuck

Students begin our class fairly well convinced that it is not possible to adjust the hectic pace of their lives. They don't see any way of finding a less stressful, healthier way to live. It doesn't even occur to them that changing the way they think about their lives would be a useful exercise. As they participate in the course, they begin to realize that they are not prisoners of their thoughts and feelings. The mindfulness training helps them gain the distance that comes when you step out of the flood onto the riverbank and watch your thoughts. Students commonly say that they now feel able to manage challenges that previously kept them stuck.

- "It's much easier to let go of negative thoughts that used to stick with me throughout the day."
- "I have skills to steer my life and to take charge of the way I live and the way I feel."
- "I will notice much more [of] what is going on around me in my present moment. I think it has also given me a way to observe rather than try to deny feelings of loss/sadness."
- "I hope I will actually be present for my life, now."
- "A comment of the teacher from last week really resonated with me: how it is really common for students to think [that] 'after this semester, after this degree, then I'll start living the life I want to lead' and how, before you know it, a lifetime has passed you by. So, I've really been making a point to live a more balanced life now instead of saying, 'once I graduate, I'll start eating healthy, etc."
- "Eating meditation was particularly helpful; incorporating this could literally change my life because dealing with an eating disorder has been a struggle in the past."
- "The class has brought me more awareness during a difficult time in my life. I will continue to practice to deepen the experience. I am glad I did this class because it will help me change my lifestyle."

I Can Manage My Relationships More Thoughtfully

In class we frequently hear students proudly relate how they managed a tense interaction with another person. They say, for example, that they were able to keep their awareness in the present and respond from that perspective. Again, this is a core teaching of mindfulness: to respond rather than react.

- "I have begun to recognize patterns of thought, particularly in relation to making lists/plans and eating. I also hope to be a more compassionate person if I can recognize my feelings of judgment and animosity towards others."
- "[I will] keep working to respond mindfully rather than react in crisis situation[s]. To accept moments, situations, people as they are rather than as I wish them to be."
- "I'm grateful for this opportunity. I did not have a good thanksgiving holiday because there were several bad things happening in my family. The practice made me able to calm down and face that."
- "This [class] changed my life. I really enjoyed becoming aware of the power of awareness in relationships, mental health, and happiness."

I Am Not So Overwhelmed or Anxious; I Have Tools to Help Me Deal with Difficult Feelings and Situations

A unique aspect of the model you are learning is that it teaches several skills that can bring immediate relief from stress and anxiety, including belly breathing, dynamic breathing, and guided imagery. These skills can be used at any time. Belly breathing can even be used in a classroom or an interpersonal situation. Students confirm that these strategies are effective for helping them manage their stress.

- "I have a tool (breathing) to better deal with small anxiety attacks."
- "With belly breathing, sleeping is much better now. I found a way to relax before going to sleep."
- "I am already responding differently to stressful situations. I think I will continue to use the techniques I learned in these situations as well as in daily practice."
- "Dynamic breathing is something I think I can use a lot to help me."
- "I particularly loved the guided imagery exercise. I've already felt some of the benefits of these techniques and expect they will be even more rewarding as I grow and progress with them Thanks you, guys!"
- "I enjoy the guided imagery for stress reduction."
- "Walking meditation is awesome for anxiety."
- "The gatha [is] particularly helpful, especially when I am meditating on my own and can't seem to focus or decide which type of meditation I should be doing."
- "Thanks for teaching me these important coping skills! I've noticed significant improvement in mental health. I feel this course has kept me from having to increase [the use of] antidepressants and may help me stop using my current dose."

Final Thoughts

Our experience has proved our initial instinct to be correct: emerging adults are perfect candidates for training in mindfulness and meditation. Our students have incorporated their mindfulness skills in meaningful ways that will contribute to their growth and health as they transition to full adulthood. As teachers, we have found our work with our students to be tremendously rewarding. Emerging adults are an amazing group and a delight to work with. They transform so willingly and joyfully, and we teachers have the privilege of participating in that transformation.

We believe that the "mindfulness shift" will be with our students for the rest of their lives; they will always have access to the potential that lies within the present moment. However, we also know that without continued support, their mindfulness practice is unlikely to deepen further and prepare them even more fully for life's inevitable challenges. We strongly encourage them to find a practice group, to read further, and to try workshops and retreats. But in the end, like all teachers, we must let them go and trust that they will find their way.

> This class has really made a positive impact on my life in every day moments. I feel all the wiser and happier. Thank you for revealing to me the gift of mindfulness meditation. — a Duke student

Center for Mind–Body Medicine

Founded in 1991 by James S. Gordon, M.D., the Center for Mind–Body Medicine is a nonprofit organization that "is working to create a more effective, comprehensive and compassionate model of healthcare and health education. The Center's model combines the precision of modern science with the wisdom of the world's healing traditions, to help health professionals heal themselves, their patients and clients, and their communities" (from its Web site: http://www.cmbm.org).

The Center has taken its mind–body skills program to many traumatized areas of the world, including Bosnia, Kosovo, the Gaza strip, and Haiti. Studies have come out of its work, such as that of Gordon, Staples, Byta, Bytyqi, and Wilson (2008). In this study, 82 adolescents were divided into two groups; one group received mind–body skills training, and the other was put on a waiting list. Symptoms of posttraumatic stress disorder were measured before and after the training. The students in the training group showed a significant reduction in their symptoms compared to those in the other group.

The Center's fundamental training takes place in mind–body skills groups. In small groups, the participants learn and practice mindfulness meditation, guided imagery, biofeedback and autogenic training, breathing and movement, and self-expression through drawings and words. The format of Koru is based on the Center's model.

Syllabus for Koru: A Course for Teaching Mindfulness and Meditation to Students

Welcome! We hope that this class will be meaningful for you as you learn more about yourselves and how to use mindfulness-based skills and meditation to manage stress and improve your general quality of life.

> If we can take a stand here, and let go into the full texture of now, we may find that this very moment is worthy of our trust. From such experiments, conducted over and over again, may come a new sense that somewhere deep within us resides a profoundly healthy and trustworthy core, and that our intuitions, as deep resonances of the actuality of the present moment are worthy of our trust.

> Jon Kabat-Zinn, *Wherever You Go, There You Are* (1994, p. 59)
> Copyright ©1994 Jon Kabat-Zinn, Ph.D. Reprinted by
> Permission of Hyperion. All Rights Reserved.

Some Requests

Please let us know if you won't be able to attend a class.
Please turn off pagers and cell phones before coming to the class.
Please be punctual! We will end the class promptly at 6:30 p.m.
In order to deepen your learning, we ask you to:

- fill in your log daily and bring it to the next class
- practice a skill/meditation for at least 10 minutes every day
- read the required chapters in the book

Schedule of Classes

Class 1: breathing exercises
Class 2: walking meditation
Class 3: guided imagery
Class 4: eating meditation

Description of Skills
Breathing

Belly or Diaphragmatic Breathing

Sit or lie down in a comfortable position. Place one hand on your abdomen in order to feel it rising and falling. Bring your focus/awareness to your breathing. In order to deepen and slow your breathing, you may wish to count to 4 as you inhale, making sure that your abdomen is rising, and then exhale to a count of 4.

Dynamic Breathing

This is easier to do standing. Keeping your mouth closed, breathe quickly and deeply. Placing your fists at armpit level, use your arms as bellows, pumping as you breathe; on your exhalation your arms are pushing at your chest. Breathe as rapidly as you can but also deeply. Try not to tense your neck and shoulders. Do this for just a few minutes. After you stop, you may want to put on some dance music and move freely for a few minutes to the music.

Walking Meditation

Find a place where you can walk comfortably back and forth for 10–30 steps. Begin with standing, centering yourself, and closing your eyes. Feel the bottom of your feet. Then open your eyes and walk very slowly, with a sense of ease and dignity. With each step, feel the sensation of lifting each foot off the floor. Be aware as you place each foot on the floor. Feel each step mindfully. When you reach the end of your path, pause, center yourself, and carefully turn around. You can experiment with the speed, walking at whatever pace keeps you most present.

Guided Imagery

Assume any kind of relaxing position and close your eyes. Bring your attention to your breathing, and let it be even and comfortable. Now, see yourself in a very special place, a place in which you feel completely comfortable and safe. Appreciate it with all of your senses. Hear the sounds, smell the aromas, feel the air and ground. Notice what you are wearing, what time of year it is and what time of day, how old you are, whether you are alone, what colors are visible, and what the temperature is.

Look around to see if there is anything else that would make this place more safe for you, perhaps something you need to remove or add. And take time to enjoy this feeling of safety in your special place. Thank yourself for taking this time and reassure yourself that you will visit this place or some other place on your own whenever you need to do so.

Eating Meditation

Prepare to take a bite and first look carefully at the food, noting its shape and color. Notice your body: Are you salivating? How does your body anticipate eating this food? And now, be aware as your arm brings the food to your mouth. Experience the food in your mouth. Chew slowly and focus fully on the taste and texture. Notice what you feel as you prepare to swallow. Swallow and notice how far into your body you can feel the food as it goes down.

Resources

- Calming music: "Alina" by Arvo Pärt, CDs by Steven Halpern, flute music by R. Carlos Nakai
- *The Relaxation and Stress Reduction Workbook* by Martha Davis, Elizabeth Robbins Eshelman, and Matthew McKay
- *A Mindfulness-Based Stress Reduction Workbook* by Bob Stahl and Elisha Goldstein
- Center for Mind–Body Medicine: http://www.cmbm.org
- Good books on mindfulness by Stephen Levine, Cheri Huber, Eckhart Tolle, Thich Nhat Hanh, Bhante Ghunaratana, Pema Chōdrōn, and Sharon Saltzberg
- CD sets and other books by Kabat-Zinn

Reading

Please read at least the following parts of the text for this course, Jon Kabat-Zinn's *Wherever You Go, There You Are* (1994):

For class 2: pp. 1–34, 101–134, 145–148
For class 3: pp. 35–99
For class 4: pp. 195–216

Daily Log for Mindfulness and Meditation

Name: _____

Daily life mindfulness activity for the week: _____

	DATE	MINDFULNESS EXERCISE	MINUTES OF PRACTICE	I'M GRATEFUL FOR . . .
Tuesday				1. 2.
Wednesday				1. 2.
Thursday				1. 2.
Friday				1. 2.
Saturday				1. 2.
Sunday				1. 2.
Monday				1. 2.

E-mails

First E-Mail: Confirmation of Enrollment in Koru

Koru is the Maori word for the unfurling fern frond. It symbolizes balanced growth. The spiral shape reflects perpetual movement around a center of stable, authentic values.

Hello and welcome:

You are receiving this message because you have registered for Koru, a program offered by Counseling and Psychological Services (CAPS) for teaching mindfulness and meditation to Duke students. This class has proven very popular with Duke students over the last few years, and we expect that you will enjoy it and find it useful. Margaret Maytan and Holly Rogers will be teaching the class, and we are looking forward to meeting you and helping you get started with a mindfulness practice.

The course meets on Tuesdays from 4:30 to 5:45 on four dates: September 27, October 4, October 18, and October 25.

Attendance at all four classes is required, so please double-check your schedules and make sure that these dates work for you. **Once you've checked your dates, please reply to this e-mail and confirm whether you still plan to attend the course.**

The text for the class is Jon Kabat-Zinn's *Wherever You Go, There You Are* (1994). This is available at the Gothic Bookstore in the Bryan Center or on Amazon.com. You might want to get the book now to familiarize yourself with some of the ideas we'll be teaching in the class.

We'll be sending out more information when it gets closer to the time to start the class. Please let us know if you have any questions at all about the course.

Take care,

Holly and Margaret

The very act of stopping, of nurturing moments of non-doing, of simply watching, puts you on an entirely different footing vis-à-vis the future. How? Because it is only by being fully in this moment that any future moment might be one of greater understanding, clarity and kindness, one less dominated by fear or hurt and more by dignity and acceptance.

Jon Kabat-Zinn: *Wherever You Go, There You Are* (1994, p. 224)

Second E-Mail: Before the First Class

[date]

Greetings, everyone!

Well, it's time to start "Koru: Mindfulness and Meditation for Duke Students"!

We are very much looking forward to meeting each of you. Class begins on September 27, 4:30–5:45 p.m. at CAPS (above Page Auditorium, Room 217). Please be punctual, and please let us know if you can't attend. You can e-mail Margaret by replying to this e-mail or call CAPS at 660-1000.

All you need to bring are willingness and openness. And please bring a short quote from the book (*Wherever You Go, There You Are*) to share with the class.

In the meantime, here is a quote for your reflection:

Mindfulness means paying attention in a particular way: on purpose, in the moment, and nonjudgementally. This kind of attention nurtures greater awareness, clarity, and acceptance of present-moment reality. It wakes us up to the fact that our lives unfold only in moments. If we are not fully present for many of those moments, we may not only miss what is most valuable in our lives but also fail to realize the richness and the depth of our possibilities for growth and transformation.

Jon Kabat-Zinn, *Wherever You Go, There You Are* (1994, p. 4)

With warm greetings,

Holly and Margaret

Third E-Mail: Between the First and Second Classes

Hello, everyone!

Meditation, and especially mindfulness meditation, is not the throwing of a switch and catapulting yourself anywhere, nor is it entertaining certain thoughts and getting rid of others. Nor is it making your mind blank or willing yourself to be peaceful or relaxed. It is really an inward gesture that inclines the heart and mind toward a full-spectrum awareness of the present moment just as it is, accepting whatever is happening simply because it is already happening. . . .

JON KABAT-ZINN, *Coming to Our Senses* (2005, p. 61)

Hope you enjoyed the class as much as we did; what a great group! We believe we're all going to learn from each other.

We covered a lot in just 1 hour, with deep belly breathing, dynamic breathing, body scan meditation, and meditation focusing on the breath. Whew! Don't worry if you didn't "get it" all. It takes practice, and the point is to just do it, without judging, as best you can. Try different things during this week.

Mindfulness is simply learning to focus the mind and awareness in the current moment's activity. Our daily life consists of only such moments, and you will learn to be more and more mindful in your daily lives. Several everyday activities that were mentioned in class are good times to practice being mindful: washing dishes, brushing your teeth, showering, etc. And hopefully, we are building into our lives a 10-minute daily meditation practice, which can permeate our whole day and help in our mindfulness practice.

Please read the assigned pages of the book before our next class.

Hope you will practice as much as you can, and we wish you all a refreshing week!

Another Example of a Third E-Mail

Hi, everyone!

What a wonderful class on Tuesday! We hope you all enjoyed it as much as we did and perhaps learned something!

And thanks to all of you for being on time. Since we only have a little over an hour, this means a lot.

How is practice going? Is the book helpful?

Here's an idea: see if you can take a shower and keep your mind on what the shower feels like in your body instead of doing all the other things we do in the shower—planning, worrying, etc. And of course, when the mind wants to do all that stuff, just bring it back gently and nonjudgmentally to the sensations in your body.

Fourth E-Mail: Between the Second and Third Classes

Hi, everyone!

Another great class! Can you feel how we all are enriched together in our practice? We are grateful for your openness and willingness to engage in this process.

Has anybody tried walking meditation this week? Remember, you can even RUSH mindfully! And how about trying the chaotic/dynamic breathing?

Someone asked us, if we're bringing ourselves back to the present moment over and over, what about planning? Well, this practice isn't about *not* planning; it's about doing whatever you're doing with awareness and as mindfully as you can. That includes planning!

> It is possible through meditation to find shelter from much of the wind that agitates the mind. Over time, a good deal of the turbulence may die down from lack of continuous feeding. But ultimately the winds of life and of the mind will blow, do what we may. Meditation is about knowing something about this and how to work with it.
>
> Jon Kabat-Zinn, *Wherever You Go, There You Are* (1994, p. 31)

> Although it is tempting to do so, you can't just think that you understand how to be mindful and save using it for only those moments when the big events hit. They contain so much power they will overwhelm you instantly, along with all your romantic ideas about equanimity and how to be mindful. Meditation practice is the slow, disciplined work of digging trenches, of working in the vineyards, of bucketing out a pond. It is the work of moments and the work of a lifetime, all wrapped into one.
>
> Jon Kabat-Zinn, *Wherever You Go, There You Are* (1994, p. 111)

See you next week; enjoy the weather this weekend.

Fifth and Final E-Mail: After the Third Class

Hello!

It is hard to believe that our final class is coming up in a few days! We hope that the week is going well for you and that you are continuing your practice. Has anyone tried using guided imagery?

Please bring another quote from the book with you for class, something that is meaningful for you!

Here are some quotes from Kabat-Zinn's book *Coming to Our Senses* (2005):

"Meditation is a way of being, not a technique. . . ." (p. 58)

"Meditation is not relaxation spelled differently. . . ." (p. 58)

"From the point of view of awareness, any state of mind is a meditative state. Anger or sadness is just as interesting and useful and valid to look at as enthusiasm or delight, and far more valuable than a blank mind, a mind that is insensate, out of touch." (p. 62)

"One approach is to think of meditation as instrumental, a method, a discipline that allows us to cultivate, refine and deepen our capacity to pay attention and to dwell in present-moment awareness. . . . The other way of describing meditation is that whatever 'meditation' is, it is not instrumental at all, it is not a doing. There is no going anywhere, nothing to practice, no beginning, middle or end, no attainment and nothing to attain. . . . These two descriptions inform each other. When we hold them both, even merely conceptually at first, then the effort we make at sitting, or in the body scan or the yoga, or in bringing mindfulness into all aspects of our lives, will be the right kind of effort." (pp. 64, 65, 67)

How is your practice going? Please keep filling in the logs and reading the book. You should be almost finished with the book.

Those 10 minutes a day for yourself and your meditation practice may be hard to find, but just keep trying and notice your own resistance without judging yourself. Remember: you can use any type of meditation/skill each day—the two kinds of breathing, the guided meditations, just being still and following your breath.

All the best, and see you next week. Hard to believe it will be our last class!

Meditation and Mindfulness: Next Steps Guide

(What follows is a template for you to use as you plan your own next steps list.)

Join a Sitting Group or Class

This will be the most critical step for your continued practice of mindfulness. There are so many cultural pulls away from this practice that if you don't spend some time on a regular basis with others who are practicing, you're likely to lose your momentum. Here are suggestions to consider.

1. Check the CAPS Web site each semester. We often offer refresher class for students who have already taken Koru.
2. Look for a meditation group on campus. The Duke Buddhist Community has three meditation groups each week. Students interested in secular meditation or other religious traditions are always welcome to attend. The Oasis on campus often offers meditation opportunities. Search campus Web sites for other options.
3. Consider community meditation groups. There are multiple meditation groups in Durham. Most of them are oriented toward Buddhist philosophy, but you certainly don't have to be Buddhist or even particularly interested in Buddhism to attend.
4. Register for a Mindfulness-Based Stress Reduction training program. This is an 8-week course for learning mindfulness meditation developed by Jon Kabat-Zinn. Both Duke and the University of North Carolina have excellent programs.

Read Another Book

Continuing to read about mindfulness is a good way to expand your knowledge and keep yourself motivated. Consider trying one of the books listed below, or go to your favorite bookstore and browse until you find one that interests you.

1. *Mindfulness for Beginners* by Kabat-Zinn (2012). If you like Kabat-Zinn's style, you might want to try another book by him. This one is similar to *Wherever You Go, There You Are* but illuminates a beginner's practice in different ways and also includes CDs with meditations.
2. *Coming to Our Senses* by Jon Kabat-Zinn (2005). This book addresses the practice of mindfulness in the context of fundamental issues facing humanity today. The short chapters are easily digested.
3. *Moment by Moment* by Jerry Braza. This is a very short introductory book to mindful meditation. It's easy to read and straightforward.
4. *Beginning Mindfulness* by Andrew Weiss (2004). This book includes a number of gathas for those of you who find it helpful to use those little poems.
5. *Mindfulness in Plain English* by Henepola Gunaratana. This book has a more Buddhist perspective, but it's a great introduction to mindfulness. The style is very direct and the meditation instructions are easy to follow.
6. *The Relaxation & Stress Reduction Workbook* by Martha Davis, Elizabeth Robbins Eshelman, and Matthew McKay, (2008). This book can help you with specific mind–body skills and different types of meditation. It is a manual, not a book you read from cover to cover.
7. *A Mindfulness-Based Stress Reduction Workbook* by Bob Stahl and Elisha Goldstein (2010). This workbook also includes CDs.

Use Guided Meditations

If you find it helpful to use guided meditations and visualizations, consider these options:

1. Jon Kabat-Zinn's CDs. Kabat-Zinn has a number of recorded meditations. Check out http://www.Amazon.com for a full listing.
2. iTunes. Go to iTunes and search "guided meditations" or "visualization." You'll find many free podcasts available, such as Meditation Oasis or Beginning Meditation. Probably a number of these won't suit your taste, but search until you find one that works for you. It can be really helpful to subscribe to a podcast and get new meditations on a regular basis.
3. http://www.Wildmind.org. This Web site has a number of audio meditations to choose from.

4. For guided imagery, any of Belleruth Naparstek's CDs are great. Go to httpl//:www. healthjourneys.com.

Attend a Meditation Retreat

Retreats are teacher-led intensive meditation trainings; some last for only half a day, others for several days. Retreats are by far the best way to quickly deepen your practice and take your mindfulness skills to a new level. And you now have the skills to attend a retreat! There are many retreat centers throughout the United States, so check the Web for centers near your home. You'll find that most of them are Buddhist in orientation, but again, you don't have to have a particular interest in Buddhism to attend. Here are a couple that we can recommend:

1. *Insight Meditation Society*. This center is located in Barre, Massachusetts. It has an excellent selection of retreats taught by some of the best teachers around. Get more information at http://www.dharma.org.
2. *Omega Institute for Holistic Studies*. This institute offers workshops and retreats in Rhinebeck, New York, and around the world. Go to http://www.Institute@eomega.org.
3. Often meditation teachers visit a city or university to lead retreats. Check the Web sites of local meditation groups to find information about upcoming retreats in your area.

Evaluation Form for Koru

Today's date:

1. What part of the class was most meaningful to you?

2. As a result of this class, what will you do differently in your life?

3. Was there anything you would have changed or added?

4. Please give feedback re:
    Check-in:
    Logs:
    Book:
    Meditation practice at home:
    CD:
    Specific skills (belly breathing, dynamic breathing, walking meditation, eating meditation, guided imagery, use of gatha, body scan):

5. Other feedback:

References

Arnett, J. J. (2000). Emerging adulthood: A theory of development from the late teens through the twenties. *American Psychologist, 55,* 469–480.

Arnett, J. J. (2004). *Emerging adulthood: The winding road from the late teens through the twenties.* New York: Oxford University Press.

Chickering, A. W. (1969). *Education and identity.* San Francisco: Jossey-Bass.

Chickering, A. W., & Reisser, L. (1993). *Education and identity* (2nd ed.) San Francisco: Jossey-Bass.

Dalen, J., Smith, B. W., Shelley, B. M., Sloan, A. L., Leahigh, L., & Begay, D. (2010). Pilot study: Mindful Eating and Living (MEAL): Weight, eating behavior, and psychological outcomes associated with a mindfulness-based intervention for people with obesity. *Complementary Therapy and Medicine, 18*(6), 260–264. References and further reading may be available for this article. To view references and the list of further reading, you must purchase the article.

Davidson, R. J., Kabat-Zinn, J., Schumacher, J., Rosenkranz, M., Muller, D., Santorelli, S. F., et al. (2003). Alterations in brain and immune function produced by mindfulness meditation. *Psychosomatic Medicine, 65,* 564–570.

Davis, M., Eshelman, E. & McKay, M. (2008). *The Relaxation & Stress Reduction Workbook* (6th ed). Oakland, CA: New Harbinger Publications.

Deckro, G. R., Ballinger, K. M., Hoyt, M., Wilcher, M., Dusek, J., Myers, P., et al. (2002). The evaluation of a mind/body intervention to reduce psychological distress and perceived stress in college students. *Journal of American College of Health, 50*(6), 281–287.

Deuter, G. (1990) *Osho Kundalini meditation* (CD). Ashland, OR: New Earth

Ekman, P., Davidson, R. J., &, Fieson, W. V. (1990). The Duchenne smile: Emotional expression and brain physiology. II. *Journal of Personality and Social Psychology, 58*(2), 342–353.

Feldman, G., Greeson, J., & Senville, J. (2010). Differential effects of mindful breathing, progressive muscle relaxation, and loving-kindness meditation on decentering and negative reactions to repetitive thoughts. *Behaviour Research and Therapy, 48,* 1002–1011.

Franco, C., Manas, I., Cangas, A. J., & Gallego, J. (2010). The applications of mindfulness with students of secondary school: Results on the academic performance, self-concept and anxiety. *Knowledge Management, Information Systems, E-Learning, and Sustainability Research Communications in Computer and Information Science, 111,* 83–97.

Gaudet, A. D., Ramer, L. M., Nakonechny, J., Cragg, J. J., & Ramer, M. S. (2010). Small-group learning in an upper-level university biology class enhances academic performance and student attitudes toward group work. *PLoS One, 5*(12):e15821.

Gaultney, J. (2010). The prevalence of sleep disorders in college students: Impact on academic performance. *Journal of American College of Health, 59*(2), 91–97.

Goleman, D. (1989, July 18). A feel-good theory: A smile affects mood. *New York Times*

Gordon, J. S., Staples, J. K., Byta, A., Bytyqi, M., & Wilson, A. (2008). Treatment of posttraumatic stress disorder in post-war Kosovo adolescents using mind-body skills groups: A randomized controlled trial. *Journal of Clinical Psychiatry, 69,* 1469–1476.

Greeson, J. M. (2009). Mindfulness research update: 2008. *Complementary Health Practice Review, 14*(1), 10–18.

Hahn, T. N. (1987). *Being Peace.* Berkely, CA: Parallax Press.

Hesslinger, B., Tebartz van Elst, L., Nyberg, E., Dykierek, P., Richter, H., Berner, M., et al. (2002). Psychotherapy of attention deficit hyperactivity disorder in adults. *European Archives of Psychiatry and Clinical Neuroscience, 252*(4), 177–184.

Holzel, B. K., Carmody, J., Vangel, M., Congleton, C., Yerramsetti, S. M., Gard, T., et al. (2011). Mindfulness practice leads to increases in regional brain grey matter density. *Psychiatry Research, 191*(1), 36–43.

Howe, N., & Strauss, W. (2000). *Millennials rising: The next great generation.* New York: Vintage.

Jain, S., Shapiro, S. L., Swanick, S., Roesch, S. C., Mills, P. J., Bell, I., et al. (2007). A randomized controlled trial of mindfulness meditation versus relaxation training: Effects on distress, positive states of mind, rumination, and distraction. *Annals of Behavioral Medicine, 33*(1), 11–21.

Janszky, I., Ahnve, S., Lundberg, I., & Hemmingsson, T. (2010). Early-onset depression, anxiety, and risk of subsequent coronary heart disease: 37-year follow-up of 49,321 young Swedish men. *Journal of the American College of Cardiology, 56*(1), 47–48.

Kabat-Zinn, J. (1994). *Wherever you go, there you are.* New York: Hyperion.

Kabat-Zinn, J. (2002). *Guided mindfulness meditation* (4-CD set). Boulder, CO: Sounds True.

Kabat-Zinn, J. (2005). *Coming to our senses.* New York: Hyperion.

Kabat-Zinn, J. (2006). *Mindfulness for beginners* (2-CD set). Boulder, CO: Sounds True.

Kabat-Zinn, J. (2012). *Mindfulness for beginners.* Boulder, CO: Sounds True.

Kabat-Zinn, J., Wheeler, E., Light, T., Skillings, A., Scharf, M. J., Cropley, T. G., et al. (1998). Influence of a mindfulness meditation-based stress reduction intervention on rates of skin clearing in patients with moderate to severe psoriasis undergoing phototherapy (UVB) and photochemotherapy (PUVA). *Psychosomatic Medicine, 60*(5), 625–632.

Killingsworth, M. A., & Gilbert, D. T. (2010). A wandering mind is an unhappy mind. *Science, 330*(no. 6006), 932. For supporting online material, go to http://www.sciencemag.org/cgi/content/full/330/6006/932/DC1.

Kuyken, W., Byford, S., Taylor, R. S., Watkins, E., Holden, E., White, K., et al. (2008). Mindfulness-based cognitive therapy to prevent relapse in recurrent depression. *Journal of Consulting and Clinical Psychology, 76*(6), 966–978.

Levin, T. (2011, January 26). Record levels of stress found in college freshmen. *New York Times,* p. A1.

Manzoni, G., Pagnini, F., Castelnuovo, G., & Molinari, E. (2008). Relaxation training for anxiety: A ten-year systematic review with meta-analysis. *BioMed Central Psychiatry, 8,* 41. To see the full article online, go to http://www.biomedcentral.com/1471-244X/8/41

Marois, R. (2006). Isolation of a central bottleneck of information processing with time-resolved fMRI. *Neuron, 52*(6), 1109–1120.

McGee, M. (2008). Meditation and psychiatry. *Psychiatry,* January, 28–41.

Nakai, R. C. (2003). *Canyon trilogy* (CD). Phoenix, AZ: Canyon Records.

Oman, D., Shapiro, S. L., Thoresen, C. E., Plante, T. G., & Flinders, T. (2008). Meditation lowers stress and supports forgiveness among college students: A randomized controlled trial. *Journal of American College of Health, 56*(5), 569–578.

Ong, J., & Sholtes, D. (2010). A mindfulness-based approach to the treatment of insomnia. *Journal of Clinical Psychology: In Session, 66*(11), 1175–1184.

Ophir, E., Nass, C., & Wagner, A. D. (2009). Cognitive control in media multi-taskers. *Proceedings of the National Academy of Sciences of the United States of America, 106*(37), 15583–15587.

Part, A. (1999). *Alina* (CD). Munich: ECM Records GmbH.

Proulx, K. (2008). Experiences of women with bulimia nervosa in a mindfulness-based eating disorder treatment group. *Eating Disorders, 16*(1), 52–72.

Roberts, K. C., & Danoff-Burg, S. (2010). Mindfulness and health behaviors: Is paying attention good for you? *Journal of American College of Health, 59*(3), 165–173.

Rosenzweig, S., Reibel, D. K., Greeson, J. M., Brainard, G. C., & Hojat, M. (2003). Mindfulness-based stress reduction lowers psychological distress in medical students. *Teaching and Learning in Medicine, 15*(2), 88–92.

Shapiro, S. L., Schwartz, G. E., & Bonner, G. (1998). Effects of mindfulness-based stress reduction on medical and premedical students. *Journal of Behavioral Medicine, 21*(6), 581–599.

Siegler, I. C., Petersen, B. L., Barefoot, J. C., & Williams, R. B. (1992). Hostility during late adolescence predicts coronary risk factors at mid-life. *American Journal of Epidemiology, 136*(2), 146–154.

Stahl, B., & Goldstein, E (2010). *A mindfulness-based stress reduction workbook.* Oakland, CA: New Harbinger Publications

Tang, Y.-Y., Ma, Y., Wang, J., Fan, Y., Feng, S., Lu, Q., et al. (2007). Short-term meditation training improves attention and self-regulation. *Proceedings of the National Academy of Sciences of the United States of America, 104*, 17152–17156.

Tolle, E. (1999). *The power of now: A guide to spiritual enlightenment.* Vancouver, Canada: Namaste Publishing.

Tusek, D. L., Church, J. M., Strong, S. A., & Fazio, V. W. (1997). Guided imagery: A significant advance in the care of patients undergoing elective colorectal surgery. *Diseases of the Colon and Rectum, 401*(2), 172–178.

U.S. Department of Education, National Center for Education Statistics. (2009). *Digest of Education Statistics, 2008* (NCES 2009-020), chap. 3.

Witek-Janusek, L., Albuquerque, K., Chroniak, K. R., Chroniak, C., Durazo-Arvizu, R., & Mathews, H. L. (2008). Effect of mindfulness based stress reduction on immune function, quality of life and coping in women newly diagnosed with early stage breast cancer. *Brain, Behavior, and Immunity, 22*(6), 969–981.

Yook, K., Lee, S. H., Ryu, M., Kim, K. H., Choi, T. K., Suh, S. Y., et al. (2008). Usefulness of mindfulness-based cognitive therapy for treating insomnia in patients with anxiety: A pilot study. *The Journal of Nervous and Mental Disease, 196*, 501–503.

Zajonc, R. B. (1985). Emotion and facial efference: A theory reclaimed. *Science, 228*(4695), 15–21.

Zylowska, L., Ackerman, D. L., Yang, M. H., Futrell, J. L., Horton, N. L., Hale, T.S., et al. (2008). Mindfulness meditation training in adults and adolescents with ADHD: A feasibility study. *Journal of Attention Disorders, 11*(6), 737–746.

Index